PERIODS OF TYPOGRAPHY

SPANISH SIXTEENTH-CENTURY PRINTING

BY

HENRY THOMAS, D.Litt.

Deputy Keeper of Printed Books, British Museum

With Fifty Illustrations

NEW YORK
CHARLES SCRIBNER'S SONS
1926

MADE AND PRINTED IN GREAT BRITAIN

The Mayflower Press, Plymouth. WILLIAM BRENDON & SON, LTD.

PERIODS OF TYPOGRAPHY

A Series of Handbooks to Historic Style in Printing.
Under the general editorship of STANLEY MORISON

BESIDES their fifty or so plates the volumes each contain an essay which will introduce the reader to the principal formative influences and to outstanding examples of the respective periods. The introductions, which in each case come from expert hands, are written from the standpoint of the amateur interested in the part played by the printed book in the society and culture of its period, rather than from that of the professional bibliographer and zealot for typographical minutiæ.

The Italian Sixteenth Century.   By A. F. Johnson, M.A., of the British Museum.

The Spanish Sixteenth Century.   By Henry Thomas, D.Litt., of the British Museum.

Early Basle Printing.   By A. F. Johnson, M.A., of the British Museum.

The French Eighteenth Century.   By Stanley Morison.

The English Eighteenth Century.   By Henry Thomas.

Incunabula.   By Victor Scholderer, B.A.

PERIODS OF TYPOGRAPHY

SPANISH SIXTEENTH-CENTURY PRINTING

SPANISH SIXTEENTH-CENTURY PRINTING

Spanish books of the fifteenth century have long attracted those interested in early printing quite as much as have the incunabula of any other country, and the productions of the first Spanish printing presses are well known to students and collectors, mainly through the works of Dr. Conrad Haebler, whose *Bibliografía ibérica del siglo XV* summarises the existing books and their printers, and whose more readable works, notably his *Geschichte des spanischen Frühdruckes in Stammbäumen*, published two years ago, provide a complete historical survey of this field.

Concerning Spanish printing of the sixteenth century, on the other hand, little of a general character has been written, and outside their own country Spanish books of this period are little known except to a few specialists and collectors.* Yet it is gradually becoming more widely acknowledged that Spanish printing does not abruptly lose all interest with the year 1500, that some of the finest productions of the early printing presses came from Spain, especially in the first quarter of the sixteenth century, and that the whole course of printing there during that century, as one would expect of a country with so marked an individuality, offers many points of contrast and of contact with the practice of other countries, and is well worth the attention of lovers of books and students of printing. The present brief

* Mr. D. B. Updike, in his masterly survey, *Printing Types : their History, Forms, and Use* (1922), mentions several bibliographies of the productions of separate towns, but can only refer the reader to two general works covering the century—one, the *Short-title Catalogue of Spanish Books printed before* 1601 *now in the British Museum*, the other a statistical account, *The Output of Spanish Books in the Sixteenth Century*, both by the present writer.

general survey and its accompanying illustrations are de-
signed to encourage those anxious to surmount the artificial
barrier set up by incunabulists, and to venture into the tempting
fields beyond.

Printing was introduced into Spain rather late (1474) as a
well-developed art by German craftsmen : before the end of the
fifteenth century, presses had been set up by them or by native
printers in about thirty different places. These two statements
at once suggest a few historical and geographical observations,
which may serve to explain various points in the history of
Spanish printing that might otherwise be obscure to those
unfamiliar with the Peninsula and its development.

In the first place, in 1474 Spain did not exist as the political
entity which we now know. The Peninsula was at that time
occupied by five kingdoms : the Christian kingdoms of Aragon,
Castile, Navarre, and Portugal, and the Moorish kingdom of
Granada. Yet in the very year that printing came to the land,
an event took place which foreshadowed the amalgamation of
these kingdoms realised just over a century later. In 1474
Isabella became Queen of Castile. She had married Prince
Ferdinand of Aragon five years earlier, so that when in 1479
Ferdinand succeeded to his father's throne, the two principal
kingdoms, Castile and Aragon, were united in the persons of
these " Catholic Kings." In 1492 their combined forces over-
came the Moorish kingdom of Granada, while in 1512 Ferdinand
conquered that portion of the kingdom of Navarre which lay
south of the Pyrenees. When therefore Charles I, the grandson
of Ferdinand and Isabella, succeeded to the thrones of Castile
and Aragon in 1516, the whole of Spain, as we now know it,
came under a single rule. The various elements were united
in the person of the Sovereign, who supplied the central policy;

6

but the different administrations remained, and Castile, Aragon, Catalonia, Valencia, and Navarre, for instance, each had their separate parliament.

Union within the Peninsula was followed by expansion abroad, which has a considerable bearing on our subject. In 1492, the year of the fall of Granada, Columbus discovered the New World. Castile, with its rivers running westwards and its ports facing the Atlantic, expanded on the American continent. This counterbalanced the Aragonese expansion that had long been taking place in the Mediterranean. By 1428 the Balearic Islands, Sardinia and Sicily formed part of the Aragonese dominions. During the latter half of the fifteenth century the kingdom of Naples, comprising the southern half of Italy, had been under an Aragonese prince, the bastard son of its conqueror, Alfonso V. After some transference of ownership about the turn of the century, it was conquered by Ferdinand the Catholic and annexed to Aragon by 1505. Spain was thus led to contend with France for dominion in Italy. In 1519 Ferdinand's grandson Charles lost his paternal grandfather the Emperor Maximilian; he thereupon succeeded to the Austrian dominions, including the Netherlands, and contended with France for the hegemony of Europe. Charles, now the Emperor Charles V, added the Duchy of Milan to his Italian possessions, investing his son Philip with it in 1540. Sixteen years later (1556) he abdicated, and the Spanish and Austrian dominions were split up. Charles's son and successor in Spain, Philip II, retained the Mediterranean and Italian possessions, the Franche-Comté, the Netherlands, and the territory acquired in the New World. He forcibly united Portugal with Spain in 1580; but the Northern Provinces of the Netherlands renounced their allegiance to him in 1581. Except for this, the Spanish posses-

7

sions remained unchanged till about the middle of the seventeenth century, Portugal achieving its independence first in 1640.

Charles V's vast European possessions involved him in enormous undertakings outside Spain. For the greater part of his time he was absent from the Peninsula on various European campaigns. This was not without effect for one aspect of our subject. There could be no settled Court, no regular royal residence, and so there was no recognised capital during his reign. The present capital of Spain, Madrid, had not established itself at the beginning of the period we are considering. There were, as stated above, separate parliaments for Castile, Navarre, Aragon, Catalonia and Valencia, and these met at various local centres: from the beginning of the sixteenth century to the year 1556, when Charles abdicated, the principal meeting-places of the Castilian parliament were Valladolid (ten times), Madrid (five times), Burgos (four times), and Toledo (three times). Charles' successor, Philip II, had spent a good deal of his early manhood away from Spain, Queen Mary of England claiming some portion of his time. He returned to Spain in 1559, from which year his personal government dates, and in 1560 he established Madrid as the *única corte*, the sole capital, and so it has remained ever since, except for the brief period when the Court was transferred to Valladolid at the beginning of the seventeenth century.

This non-existence of an official capital previous to the second half of the sixteenth century must be borne in mind when considering early Spanish printing. It explains the lateness of the introduction of printing into Madrid. It helps to explain the absence of any city in the Peninsula with a preponderating output, corresponding to London for England, and Paris for

France. The ultimate reason for this, however, lies in the geographical conditions of the country, whose average altitude is the second highest in Europe. The central portion consists of high tablelands cut off from each other by lofty mountain ridges, and deeply carved by large but generally unnavigable rivers. Communication by road between the different districts was, and in some cases still is, bad. We shall therefore not expect, as a rule, to find the art of printing spreading in Spain along the rivers and the trade-routes, as it did in and from Germany. We shall rather expect to find it establishing itself in the principal cities of well-defined districts. For geographical, as well as for political reasons, we shall not expect to find any city with a preponderating output.

With this preparation we may turn our attention to early Spanish printing, and to our real subject, Spanish printing in the sixteenth century. During the first quarter of a century in which printing was practised in Spain, presses were set up in about thirty different places, and these presses produced, as we may infer from the surviving specimens, about a thousand books. We need only notice here the chief cities. These mostly run in pairs. Seville, in the south, and Salamanca, in the middle west, vie with each other for first place; Barcelona and Saragossa, in the north-east, take a moderate second place; while Valencia, on the east coast, and Burgos, in the north, take a good third place. Toledo, in the centre, follows by itself at a considerable distance, heading a host of stragglers, mostly from the north and north-east: Valladolid, Lérida, Montserrat, Zamora, Pamplona, Tarragona, etc.

To the thirty printing centres of the fifteenth century in Spain there were added about another thirty during the sixteenth century, while the output of books during the latter century was roughly ten times what it had been during the previous quarter of a century. It must not be assumed, of course, that printing was at any time carried on simultaneously in sixty different places throughout Spain. In some of the earliest printing centres the presses ceased to function before the end of the fifteenth century. In some of the centres established during the sixteenth century the presses were only active temporarily; in others they were not set up till late in the century. Córdoba and Madrid, for instance, both acquired printing presses in the year 1566, the ports of Bilbao and Cádiz not till 1578 and 1595 respectively; the explanation being that these places were either not so famous as they once were, or so famous as they now are, and that they long depended for their printing on neighbouring cities like Seville, Alcalá de Henares or Toledo, and Burgos.

It must be admitted that few of the new printing centres were of much importance as such; in fact, only two of them reached the first rank. This was natural, for the main districts were already well served by the chief printing centres of the fifteenth century. These, as given above,—Seville, Salamanca, Saragossa, Valencia, and Barcelona,—were of the first rank and of almost equal output in the sixteenth century; but they were rivalled by two of the new centres just mentioned: Alcalá de Henares and Madrid. It may be noted that these two places are topographically close together in the middle of Spain: typographically, however, they are far enough apart. Printing was introduced into Alcalá in 1502; the place soon came to the front as a printing centre with the founding of the University of Alcalá by Cardinal Ximenez de Cisneros in 1508; it maintained its position for the greater part of the century, declining towards the end. On the other hand, as has already been stated,

10

printing was not introduced into Madrid till 1566, shortly after it was made the capital; but its political position soon enabled it to outstrip the old-established centres, which it robbed of a good deal of their trade, especially its near neighbour Alcalá.

With all the above cities acknowledged as of the first rank on their productions over the whole century, two of the earlier centres with a small record, having accelerated their rate of production, move up to second rank. These are Toledo, the seat of the Primate of Spain, and Valladolid, which the Court often favoured before it decided definitely on Madrid. Both Toledo and Valladolid are fairly central, though on opposite sides of the central mountain chain, and both of them, like Alcalá, suffered towards the end of the century from Madrid's promotion.

One of the earlier cities of third rank, Burgos, merely retained its position during the sixteenth century. It was almost overtaken by a much younger rival, Medina del Campo, which was central and had a celebrated annual fair. Apparently for the latter reason it developed the bookseller as distinct from the printer in Spain: at a comparatively early date we find booksellers in Medina who sold books printed for them in other towns. Granada, one of the least of the fifteenth-century printing centres, but once the capital of the old Moorish kingdom in the south, achieved a respectable fourth rank during the sixteenth century; while Logroño, Pamplona, Córdoba, Tarragona, Lérida, and Huesca are the most productive of the minor centres, and are all that need be mentioned here.

This summary of the chief Spanish printing centres of the sixteenth century would be incomplete without some reference to an aspect of our subject which is, strictly speaking, outside our province in the present sketch—the printing of Spanish books abroad. Spain was the great imperialistic power in the sixteenth century, and no country could boast of so many books printed abroad in its vernacular as could Spain. It was natural that Spanish books should be printed in the New World, which was discovered and largely ruled by Spain; but in the Old World, too, Spanish books were produced in many countries. Portugal, a foreign country before 1580, when as mentioned above it was annexed to Spain, produced Spanish books before as well as during the Spanish occupation. Educated Portuguese could and did read Spanish; some Portuguese authors wrote in Spanish; while the possibilities of the Spanish market were realised by the printers and booksellers of Lisbon, Coimbra, and Evora long before a pirated edition of *Don Quixote* was issued in Lisbon within a few months of its first appearance in Madrid.

The introductory remarks will have prepared the reader for the numerous Spanish books produced in Europe outside the Peninsula. Italy, owing to its long political and religious associations with Spain,—with Spanish kings conquering large parts of the country, and with Spaniards occupying the papal throne,—had a large Spanish population of officials, soldiers, and tradesmen. For these, and for the natives anxious to perfect themselves in the language of the governing race, Spanish books were printed from early times in ten Italian cities, the chief being Venice, Rome, and Milan. But the most important of the foreign producing countries was the Netherlands, which passed into Spanish hands in 1519. The Southern Provinces remained a Spanish possession for the rest of the century and beyond, and from about the end of the third decade Antwerp, one of the great printing centres of North-Western Europe, in the production of Spanish books rivalled numerically the Spanish cities of the second rank, while some important Spanish books

12

were printed there for the first time. It not only supplied the home market, but also utilised its facilities for export, and incidentally it was the chief source from which English readers obtained their Spanish books at this time. It completely over-shadows Brussels, Louvain, Leyden, and Liége, where also a few Spanish books were printed.

The only other country which produced Spanish books in any quantity was France. Paris established a Spanish con-nexion through its famous *Horæ* at a very early date; but Lyons, being more favourably situated, has the better record as to numbers over the whole century. England produced a few Spanish books towards the end of the century, all of them printed in London except one. This last is a Spanish grammar, to which was appended Alfonso de Valdés' famous dialogue on the sack of Rome in 1527. Some of the few known copies bear a Paris imprint, but the book was really printed at the newly revived Oxford press in 1586. The Oxford printers could hardly foresee that in 1925 an American dealer would give £100 for a copy wanting the second half, which is not the least interesting portion of the book.

It only remains to add that Spanish books were occasionally printed in Germany and Switzerland, while one was printed in Bohemia, and one as far afield as Salonika, where Spanish Jews had found a refuge.

The principal foreign countries just mentioned not only pro-duced Spanish books within their own borders; they also influenced, in different ways and in varying degrees, the de-velopment of the Spanish book in its native country during the sixteenth century. It is now time to give some account of the physical features of the Spanish book, and of the changes they underwent during the period under review.

13

Printing was introduced into the Peninsula by well-trained German craftsmen, and by the end of the fifteenth century the art had passed well beyond the elementary stage in most of the cities in which presses had been established. By this time the Spanish book was far from being the standardised product with which we are now familiar; but a distinct national style had been evolved. This style maintained itself for over half a century longer, before yielding to another that gradually became general throughout Western Europe. It is all the more interesting to us now because it differed widely from the style which replaced it—virtually the modern style—and because it affords many local varieties.

The German craftsmen first set up their presses at Valencia, which they reached by the sea-route from Italy, and the earliest books produced at Valencia—as also at Barcelona and Saragossa —were in roman type, the type generally used in the country from which the printers had just come. But the roman type soon gave way to the gothic type, which was more natural both to the German printers and to the Spanish readers. Roman type was used to some extent later in the fifteenth century both at Valencia and in the Castilian cities of Salamanca, Seville, and Burgos. It was most used at Salamanca, under the influence of the great humanist Antonio de Lebrija, whose prejudice against gothic type may be inferred from his reference, in his *Gramatica sobre la lengua castellana* (ch. 2), to the "distortion" of the roman characters by the Goths during their rule in the Peninsula.

The roman type, then, though favoured by Antonio de Lebrija and the classical scholars generally, and in spite of its clearness, gave way to the "distorted" type to which the Spaniards were accustomed, and the typical Spanish book of the early sixteenth century is in gothic type, a handsome, rounded gothic

14

type of heavy appearance, which never developed the somewhat jagged look of our own Black Letter. The types, like the books in which they were used, were rather large: the average text-type measured about 100 mm. per twenty lines, with a secondary type of about 80 mm. which could be used as a text-type for smaller books. To match these types the printers favoured heavy woodcut capitals, though some printers, especially in Seville, sought after contrasts by employing a light variety as well. Decorative accessories, when used, whether border-pieces, illustrations to the text, or printers' devices, were also heavy as a rule. The result in most cases is a general balance and grave dignity which are the most striking characteristics of the Spanish book of the early sixteenth century, as well as of its predecessors. Roman type was meantime not altogether neglected, but it was mainly confined to scholarly books. Italic type was not favoured, except in conjunction with roman type.

The standard Spanish book at the opening of the sixteenth century, then, was printed in gothic type. It was usually a folio —often in double columns—or a quarto; smaller volumes— mostly devotional or school books—were rare at first. This style continued unchallenged till towards the middle of the century. With the progress of time it underwent minor changes, and throughout it provides local variations in detail—to which the gothic book lends itself much more readily than the roman book. Types, woodcut capitals, and border-pieces especially show a pleasing variety from place to place and even from press to press, and thus generally enable unsigned books to be allotted at least to their place of origin, and in most cases to their printer. This variety reflects the various foreign influences that were absorbed in forming and developing the common style, as well as the various native regional elements.

Italy, from which printing had reached Spain—although its types, both roman and italic, were not generally accepted—continued to influence the decorative side of the book—the capitals, the borders, and the cuts. This is especially noticeable in the Mediterranean cities like Barcelona and Valencia, for the sea-route between Italy and Spain was the simplest, though there were of course land routes, by which Italian printers came to Spain in the sixteenth century. As was explained above, the political connexion between the two countries grew closer as the century advanced, and, as will be seen below, Italian models prevailed in printing in Spain, as they did in various branches of Spanish literature at a later stage.

German influence was, of course, strong everywhere at the beginning of the century, as the early German printers who settled in Spain kept up their connexion with the motherland. This was facilitated by the great trade-route which led from the Rhine valley to the Rhone valley, and passed from Perpignan, then in Spain, over the Pyrenees, following the course of the Tet and Segre rivers down to the Ebro valley near Saragossa. By this same route French influence, especially that of the great printing-centre Lyons, reached Spain. But for French influence, especially that of Paris, other ways were available—those taken by the pilgrims from all over Europe to the shrine of St. James at Compostela (in great favour about the turn of the fifteenth century), which converged on Burgos. Some important Italian printers who came to Spain seem to have followed the pilgrim way.

The only other influence that remains to be mentioned is that of the Netherlands. This was not directly felt till after the first quarter of the century, by which time the Netherlands formed part of the Spanish dominions. As with Italy, the sea-route to

16

Spain was the simplest; but the routes down the Rhine valley and through Paris were both available as well, and printers and books from the Low Countries doubtless reached Spain by all three.

When once the Spanish book was standardised as described above, its interior afforded no great scope for variety. Unless books were freely illustrated, the pages of text were necessarily uniform, except for the woodcut capitals opening prominent sections, or perhaps the woodcut borders—used more rarely as time went on—enclosing a prominent page. It was the title-page which afforded the printer his opportunity, and which consequently shows plentiful variety and progressive change.

By the beginning of the sixteenth century most Spanish books had their first leaf reserved for the title (usually accompanied by the author's name). But the printer liked to make his books attractive by decorating the title-page, even though they were not otherwise illustrated. Thus the title was commonly headed by a woodcut (or occasionally by a number of woodcuts). The woodcut tended to get supported or surrounded by small border-pieces; or both woodcut and title would be framed within larger and more elaborate border-pieces. Sometimes a frame in a single piece was used; but border-pieces were preferred, for the printer could use these in different combinations as his stock increased. Later the relations between the elements composing the title-page change, as the title moves up to accommodate information formerly reserved for the colophon at the end of the book. The rise of the publisher, as distinct from the printer, hastens the development of the imprint to which we are accustomed in books of the present day. By the time this has arrived, the title-page has assumed more or less its modern

17

aspect; but the later stages of this development took place after the gothic book had had its day.

The subject of the gothic book's decline may well be introduced by a few remarks on the title and text cuts, especially the former. The favourite themes for title cuts were a portrait of the author, or in the case of a work of history or fiction, a portrait of the hero or a scene connected with the story, or in official books a coat of arms. Portraits were readily forthcoming for authors and heroes of all centuries and climes, and it is sometimes charitable to suppose that they are all equally hypothetical. There are indeed a few fine contemporary portraits that are obviously good likenesses; but the majority of portrait cuts are merely decorative, and the same cut in its time plays many parts. A fine Seville cut which in 1503 represented St. James, the patron of Spain, fighting against the Moors—he is recognisable by his halo, the emblematic sword on his breast, and the cross, sword, and cockle-shell on his pennant—was transformed twenty-two years later into Palmerin de Oliva, the hero of a chivalresque romance, by removing the distinguishing halo, swords, and cross, while leaving the cockle-shell (Plate 19); ten years later still the same cut, with the cockle-shell also removed, serves for Clarian de Landanis, the hero of another chivalresque romance. The two figures shown in Plate 7 began life as two of the early kings of Aragon in a chronicle printed at Saragossa in 1509; here they represent the Emperor Charlemagne and one of his peers, while three other cuts from the chronicle did duty as Jesse, David, and Solomon in a Missal of 1510. Even more interesting are the two cuts at the head of Cortes' third report to the Emperor Charles V, printed at Saragossa in 1523 (Plate 18). These cuts had their origin in Mainz, and they provide a good example of early printing

18

material embarking on long-distance travel. In 1505 a profusely illustrated German edition of Livy was printed at Mainz. Before 1520 the original blocks used for this edition had passed through Lyons to Saragossa, where in that year the printer G. Coci produced with their aid an illustrated Spanish edition of Livy. A large number of the illustrations are printed from two blocks arranged side by side, a comparatively small number of blocks being used throughout the work in different combinations to represent a large number of scenes. The impartial and indefatigable gentleman who volunteered as ambassador-extraordinary, whenever Livy wished to despatch a mission from or to Rome, is seen in Plate 18 offering Cortes' report to the Emperor, a confirmed turncoat who but three years before was indifferently a Roman consul or a barbarian king or chieftain. Similarly a large cut on the verso of the first leaf of the report represents Cortes sailing the Atlantic in a vessel originally made in Germany to serve either for or against the Romans in the Mediterranean. It must be added that the cuts are more suited to the contemporary Cortes than to the classical Livy for which they were made: the sense of historical perspective was not highly developed in the artists of the time.

Very effective use was made by the early Spanish printers of coats of arms for decorative purposes, especially on the title-page, but also elsewhere. The royal or imperial coat of arms usually figures on the title-page of official publications—proclamations, collections of laws, etc.—which bulk largely in the sixteenth-century output, and all the important printers had their own particular design. Ecclesiastical, regional or local, and individual coats of arms are also fairly common, and are for the most part equally decorative. A number of examples

B *

of the various kinds, usually in combination with border-pieces, will be found illustrated in the Plates.

The absence of a sense of historical perspective just referred to, which was general in renaissance times, and still more the growing failure to insist on congruity between the spiritual and the physical elements of the book, herald the decline into which Spanish printing began to fall after about the first half century of its existence. The Spanish printers of, roughly speaking, the first quarter of the sixteenth century produced books equal to the best turned out elsewhere. After that the quality of their books begins to deteriorate, more quickly in some places than in others. The standard was better maintained where the firm of one of the old masters, especially where the master himself, was long-lived; for instance, the firm of G. Coci in Saragossa, the Cromberger firm in Seville, the Junta firm in Burgos and Salamanca, Arnao Guillen de Brocar in Alcalá de Henares and elsewhere. As was natural, the decline tended to begin earlier in places where printing had been longer established. It is noticeably rapid in cities like Barcelona and Valencia, whose extra-heavy style required very careful press-work to make it successful. But the deterioration becomes general after 1530 in Spain, as in most other countries, which makes the rare exceptions the more remarkable.

Several causes combined to bring about the deterioration of the art of printing in Spain. Increased output and increased competition went hand in hand. Greater production involved the absorption into the craft of larger numbers of workmen, who had neither the training, nor the tradition, nor the opportunity of acquiring the purer taste of their predecessors. With the extension of a printer's business, his stock of types increased and became very diversified. More especially his ornamental

20

capitals and his woodcuts accumulated, till he found himself in possession of a large and motley assortment—both as to size and treatment—upon which he, or rather his compositors, drew without discrimination: some quite early Seville books, for instance, show a ruthless accumulation of odd border-pieces on the title-page. As a result, the old uniformity—the suitable blending of type, capitals, and decorations—disappeared; and this process was accentuated as Italian influences reappeared towards the middle of the century, and essentially roman and essentially gothic elements were freely mixed. An ill-assorted assembly of types, capitals, and perhaps also woodcuts, becomes characteristic of books of any length, and this could not help but corrupt the taste of all connected with the craft. The workman found less and less inducement to turn out artistic work, owing to the nature of his materials, and he allowed his press-work to deteriorate. In this he was assisted by the quality of the paper, for increased demand tended to exhaust the supply of good paper, and inferior paper had perforce to be used. On top of all this came the impoverishment of Spain through the European wars of Charles V and Philip II, for the country's wealth was drained to support the ambitious foreign policy of these Sovereigns. The economic results of this policy were already being felt during the second quarter of the century. By hastening the decline of the gothic book they expedited the reinstatement of the roman book. Between a well-printed gothic book and a well-printed roman book the question of superior legibility is largely a question of habit. When both are badly printed, the gothic book cannot compete with the roman, and the substitution of the former by the latter is only a matter of time. In Spain the substitution was facilitated by the practice of Italy, largely in Spanish occupation, and by the example and competition of the Netherlands, a Spanish possession, and, to a lesser extent, of France, where the finest printers of roman books flourished in the second quarter of the century. From these countries too—Italy, France, and the Netherlands, and during this same period—Spain began to acquire the habit of the smaller book. Smaller sizes—octavo and less—first appear with any regularity during the third decade, but they are not very numerous till towards the middle of the century; the reintroduction of roman type helped them, for roman type is much more suitable than gothic for a smaller page.

For rather more than a third of the sixteenth century, roman type had only been used for a limited number of scholarly books, and these were mostly printed in the University towns, such as Salamanca and Alcalá de Henares. From the early 'forties, however, the roman book began to thrive gradually at the expense of the gothic book. The year 1543 is a convenient date from which to trace the growing change of style. In that year there appeared in Barcelona a famous book of verse: *Las obras de Boscan y algunas de Garcilasso de la Vega.* This book, which succeeded in imposing Italian models on Spanish poetry, was appropriately printed in roman type, of a crude early Italian pattern which had occasionally been used before in Barcelona. Italian influences, which now became so strong in Spanish literature, both poetry and prose, not unnaturally affected the physical side of Spanish books. From this time onwards the roman book began to invade the province of the gothic book. The advance began earlier, and the progress was more rapid in some places than in others. The presence of Italian firms in a city—such as the Juntas and the Portonariis in Salamanca— naturally helped the roman cause there; so too did the advent of a Netherlander—like that of J. Mey to Valencia—for Spanish books printed in the Netherlands were all in roman type. By the beginning of the 'sixties the roman book was clearly prevailing over its rival. Its complete victory dates from 1566, the year in which printing presses, using roman type, were introduced into Madrid, for Madrid had recently been made the sole capital, and as such it set the fashion for the whole country. After that date, gothic books are in a small minority, for gothic type was only used for a few reprints of very popular books, to which the old tradition still clung. It may be noted that, along with roman type, italic type came into greater favour; but it is not often found alone. Its chief use is to distinguish particular sections in roman books, for italic type at once contrasts strongly with roman type in appearance and balances it well in weight.

The change from gothic to roman type involved a complete break with the established Spanish tradition; it consequently brought other changes in its train: capitals, ornaments, and illustrations had now to match type-pages of much lighter appearance. On the title-page, borders had for long tended away from the gothic towards the renaissance style—the pseudo-classical and plateresque which prevailed in other branches of Spanish art. In the rest of the book the change came rather late and was gradual, with the result that gothic and roman elements were mixed, and taste was degraded. Further, the change took place while the country was in a poor economic condition, and Spanish printing—like that of most other countries—was on the decline. As a consequence, the Spanish printers in general were not so successful with the roman book as with the gothic. They cannot compare with the French printers of the middle period of the sixteenth century, or with the Netherlands printers who won the primacy in printing after the religious wars had brought about a decline

23

in France. There were a number of printers in various places
who produced business-like roman books during the latter half
of the century; but fine books are comparatively rare, and they
are generally found to be printed for some wealthy individual,
institution, or corporation.

One last change that occurred during the sixteenth century
remains to be noted. Book-illustration had from the beginning
shared in the general decline; as time went on woodcuts became less frequent and, with rare exceptions (see, for example,
Plate 41), coarser. During the last twenty years of the century,
however, an attempt was made to raise the standard of book-
illustration by introducing new methods. Metal cuts had
occasionally been used by the early printers, but they imitated
the prevailing woodcuts. About 1580 copper-plate engravings
began to appear in Spanish books. The new method of illustration was introduced from abroad, and we find French and
Netherlands engravers working in Spain—the fine portrait of
the future Philip III shown on Plate 49 is signed by a Netherlander. Spanish engravings are not all up to this standard, but
the clearness of their lines usually sets off the rough press-work
of the books in which they are found. As a general rule, both
the press-work and the materials in Spanish books printed
around the turn of the sixteenth century are poor, and some of
the most notable books of the best period in Spanish literature
are inferior specimens of the printer's art. Spain was not alone
in this respect: among others, both Cervantes and Shakespeare
were unworthily presented to their original public.

The above general sketch of the development of Spanish
printing during the sixteenth century must now be supple-
mented by descriptions of the Plates used as illustrations. With
the exception of the frontispiece, these are all selected from

24

books in the British Museum; they are arranged chrono-
logically, to give some idea of the growth of the Spanish book
in the principal centres. The notes in the List of Plates below
will serve to introduce the reader to as many of the chief
sixteenth-century printers as the limited material allows.

LIST OF THE PLATES

Plate 1 (Frontispiece). A sixteenth-century Spanish printing press, now in the Museo Provincial, Gerona.

Plates 2 and 3. Ludolphus de Saxonia: Vita Christi. Stanislao Polono, Alcalá de Henares, 1502–1503. Pt. 1, title-page, and pt. 2, fol. ii recto. Reduced from 245 × 170 mm. and 262 × 172 mm.

This handsome book, in four large volumes, is the first book printed in Alcalá de Henares. The printer, a Pole, came from Seville, where he had been printing since 1491. The title-page combines two of the usual ornamental motives—a topical woodcut and the royal arms. The former depicts the author presenting a volume of his work to the " Catholic Kings," Ferdinand and Isabella ; the latter incorporates the emblem of Granada, reconquered by those Sovereigns in 1492. The printer brought his types and woodcut capitals from Seville.

Plate 4. Compilacion de los establecimientos de la orden de cavalleria de Santiago del Espada. J. Pegnicer, Seville, 1503. Sig. b 1 recto. Reduced from 225 × 145 mm.

The printer, Johann Pegnitzer, was a German who had practised in Seville since 1490. The woodcut capitals, white on black, in this and the preceding plate, are naturally somewhat similar in style. Here the " P " encloses an appropriate figure of St. James. The compositor's care over the make-up of his page is shown by the bridge of text between the two columns, to support the rather broad capital.

Plate 5. Marquilles, J. de. Comentaria super usaticis Barchiñ. J. Luschner, Barcelona, 1505. Fol. 1 recto. Reduced from 253 × 178 mm.

The plate shows the heavy style of woodcut favoured in the eastern coast towns, as well as characteristic Barcelona types and capitals. The printer, a German, had worked at Barcelona or Montserrat since 1495, and had printed several Service-books—hence his miscellaneous border-pieces, which, however, are here well composed.

Plate 6. Tovar, F. Libro de musica. J. Rosenbach, Barcelona, 1510. Fol. xxvi recto. Reduced from 219 × 140 mm.

Johann Rosenbach had worked in Barcelona and elsewhere since 1492—partly in association with his compatriot Luschner. He had a long career, and printed many fine books of very individual character in Barcelona, Tarragona, Perpignan, and Montserrat. The present book is interesting because the musical notes are supplied in manuscript, as in some of the printer's Service-books, though music had been printed in Seville as early as 1492, as well as in several other places a little later.

Plate 7. Romance del conde Dirlos. [G. Coci, Saragossa, c. 1510.] Sig. a i recto.

A simple print of a popular ballad—perhaps the earliest single issue of a Spanish ballad that has survived—from the press of Georg Coci, a German, who took over a renowned Saragossa press at the end of the fifteenth century, and made it one of the most renowned presses of the sixteenth century.

The type is the favourite Saragossa text-type of the period. For remarks on the woodcut figures, see above, p. 18.

Plate 8. Petrarch. Los seys triunfos. Arnao Guillen de Brocar, Logroño, 1512. Title-page. Reduced from 243 × 153 mm.

The printer, of uncertain nationality, began work at Pamplona in 1492 (or earlier), and practised later at Logroño, Valladolid, Alcalá de Henares, Burgos, and Toledo. He was one of the most prolific and, as will be seen later, one of the most justly famous printers of the early sixteenth century.

The title-page of the present book shows the use, above the title, of a very decorative coat of arms, that of the Count Fadrique Enriquez de Cabrera, Admiral of Castile—hence the chain of anchors surrounding the arms.

Plate 9. Question de amor. D. de Gumiel, Valencia, 1513. Title-page. Reduced from 267 × 153 mm.

The printer, Diego de Gumiel, is the first undoubted Spaniard to figure in this list. He began work at Barcelona in 1494, passing from there to Valladolid and afterwards to Valencia. He used very handsome woodcut capitals, white on black background, and a similar device (see Plate 50).

The book is an early *roman à clef*, as is indicated at the end of the title : la mayor parte de la obra es istoria verdadera. Narrow border-pieces appear on both sides of the woodcut above the title.

Plate 10. Virgil: Opera omnia. G. Coci, Saragossa, 1513. Sigs. L 8 verso and M 1 recto. Reduced from 159 × 75 and 163 × 90 mm.

> For the printer, see note to Plate 7. Coci selected a roman type for this classical author, and was as successful with it as he was with his gothic types.

Plate 11. The Complutensian Polyglot Bible. Arnao Guillen de Brocar, Alcalá de Henares, 1514–1517. Title-page to the first part of the Old Testament. Reduced from 268 × 206 mm.

> This, the first polyglot Bible, was promoted by Cardinal Ximenez de Cisneros, who entrusted the printing to Brocar, calling him for that purpose to Alcalá, where he had recently founded a University. The successful carrying through of his task places Brocar in the front rank of printers of all time.
>
> The title-page reproduced shows the title and the Cardinal's coat of arms enclosed within a frame of woodcuts and border-pieces. This title-page is a special one found in very few copies.

Plate 12. Musaeus. Ποιημάτιον τα κατ' Ἐρώ καὶ Λέανδρον. [Arnao Guillen de Brocar, Alcalá de Henares, 1514.] Last page.

> Printed in the Greek type cut for the polyglot New Testament. This bold type was based on old Greek manuscripts; it departed altogether from the evil Aldine model in general use, which was based on contemporary cursive and highly contracted Greek handwriting. The Alcalá type was copied in recent times by Mr. Robert Proctor for his reprints of Aeschylus and Homer.

Plate 13. Aureum opus regalium priuilegiorum Valentiae. D. de Gumiel, Valencia, 1515. Title-page. Reduced from 242 × 162 mm.

> A fine example of the use of local arms—those of the old kingdom of Valencia —as a title-page decoration. The treatment in white on black background was much favoured by this printer, for whom see note to Plate 9.

29

Plate 14. Ciruelo, P. Cursus quatuor mathematicarum artium liberalium. Arnao Guillen de Brocar, Alcalá de Henares, 1516. Book 2, sig. B 4 recto. Reduced from 252 × 162 mm.

A skilfully printed book for the Schools—hence the roman type, in conjunction with which italic type might have been expected instead of gothic. The diagrams follow the fashion set by Ratdolt at Venice. For the printer, see note to Plate 8.

Plate 15. La cronica del conde Fernan Gonçales. Fadrique Aleman, Burgos, 1516. Sig. b 4 verso.

The printer, Friedrich Biel, originally from Basel, began work in Burgos in 1485, the present book being produced towards the end of his career.

The book is a popular history of a local hero, and the page shown is illustrated in a manner typical of Burgos books of this size for about half a century.

Plate 16. Perez de Guzman, F. Cronica del rey don Juan el Segundo. Arnao Guillen de Brocar, Logroño, 1517. Sig. B 8 verso. Reduced from 273 × 191 mm.

Shortly after printing the polyglot Bible at Alcalá de Henares, Brocar (for whom see note to Plate 8) printed this handsome book at his Logroño office by command of the Emperor Charles V, who made him the royal printer.

The page shown faces the opening of the text ; it is one of three fully illustrated pages in the book.

Plate 17. Libro de medicina llamado Compendio de la salud humana. Jacobo Cromberger, Seville, 1517. Sig. g 2 verso. Reduced from 210 × 139 mm.

Jacobo Cromberger, another German, is the first purely sixteenth-century printer to figure in this list : he continued from 1503 the Seville press of Stanislao Polono, with whom he became associated the year before. He and his son built up the best and most enterprising firm in the south of Spain, which was responsible for introducing the art of printing into America.

The page shown is in the favourite Seville text-type ; it illustrates the statement on p. 15 above as to the " contrasty " woodcut capitals used by the Seville printers.

Plate 18. Cortes, H. Carta de relacion. G. Coci, Saragossa, 1523. Title-page. Reduced from 238 × 157 mm.

For the printer, see note to Plate 7, and for the woodcuts on both sides of the first leaf of this book, see above, p. 18.

Plate 19. Palmerin de Oliva. J. Varela, Seville, 1525. Title-page. Reduced from 265 × 166 mm.

Juan Varela, a native of Salamanca, was printing in Granada early in 1505, perhaps late in 1504. He afterwards printed in Toledo, as well as in Seville, in which latter city he was a worthy rival of the Crombergers.
For remarks on the title-page cut, see above, p. 18.

Plate 20. Las notas del Relator. A. de Melgar, Burgos, 1525. Title-page. Reduced from 218 × 150 mm.

Alonso de Melgar, who printed in Burgos from 1519 to 1525, doubtless forms the connecting link in that city between two more famous printers, Friedrich Biel, already mentioned, and Juan de Junta, mentioned below.
The title-page shows the title within a single-piece renaissance frame which balances the gothic type well. This frame had belonged to Melgar's predecessor, "Fadrique Aleman," as the device in the lower section proves. Particulars as to place and date of printing here occur on the title-page.

Plate 21. Gamaliel. J. Joffre, Valencia, 1525. Fol. lxxviii verso.

Juan Joffre began printing in 1502 at Valencia, where he was one of the chief printers for more than a quarter of a century.
The page reproduced shows a miscellaneous collection of border-pieces, but neatly arranged, round the main cut—the Flight into Egypt.

Plate 22. Fernandez de Oviedo y Valdes, G. De la natural historia de las Indias. R. de Petras, Toledo, 1526. Title-page. Reduced from 245 × 158 mm.

Ramon de Petras printed a number of good books at Toledo in the short period 1524–1527. The title-page of the most important of these is here reproduced.
The title, with the imperial arms above it, is enclosed within four renaissance border-pieces, of a kind which became common in various places about this time.

c

31

Plate 23. Manuale secundum consuetudinem ecclesie Salmanticensis. J. de Junta, Salamanca, 1532. Fol. xx verso. Reduced from 189 × 120 mm.

Juan de Junta belonged to the celebrated Florentine family of printers. He came via Lyons to Spain, where he appears to have taken over the Burgos business of A. de Melgar in 1526 (see note to Plate 20). He started another press in Salamanca in 1532. Members of the Junta family continued printing in Burgos and Salamanca till late in the century.

The Manual was the first book printed by Juan de Junta in Salamanca. The page shown illustrates the style of the moderate-sized Service-book, with printed musical notes, in use at this time.

Plate 24. Tomich, P. Historias e conquestas dels excellentissims e catholics Reys de Arago. C. Amoros, Barcelona, 1534. Title-page. Reduced from 261 × 165 mm.

Carlos Amoros, a native of Provence, began printing in Barcelona in 1509, and produced, among other books, a number of official local publications between that date and 1554.

The title-page reproduced shows the arms of Aragon below the title, the whole enclosed in four border-pieces. Cf. note to Plate 22.

Plate 25. Josephus. De belo judayco. Juan Cromberger, Seville, 1536. Title-page. Reduced from 257 × 168 mm.

The printer was first partner and then successor to Jacobo Cromberger, who was no doubt his father. See note to Plate 17.

The title is enclosed within rather light borders—previously used in a 1532 edition of the same work and in a 1535 edition of *La historia general de las Indias*—contrasting with the heavy type. Cromberger at this time generally used borders similar to those shown in Plates 22, 24 and 26.

Plate 26. Beuter, P. A. Primera part de la historia de Valencia. [F. Diaz Romano,] Valencia, 1538. Title-page. Reduced from 266 × 163 mm.

Francisco Diaz Romano succeeded Juan Joffre (see note to Plate 21) in 1528, and printed in Valencia till the end of the next decade.

Above the title are the arms of Valencia, the whole being surrounded by four border-pieces—the Valencian variants of the pattern seen in Plates 22 and 24.

Plate 27. Aranzel de los derechos que han de llevar los escrivanos. Juan de Brocar, Alcalá de Henares, 1543. Title-page. Reduced from 249 × 157 mm.

Juan de Brocar succeeded in 1538 to the Alcalá and Logroño businesses of his father, Arnao Guillen de Brocar, for whom see note to Plate 8.

The title-page is mostly taken up by one of the elaborate forms of the imperial arms used in official publications during the middle period of the century.

Plate 28. Boscan Almogaver, J. Las obras de Boscan y algunas de Garcilasso de la Vega. C. Amoros, Barcelona, 1543. Fol. xix recto.

For the printer, see note to Plate 24. For the book and type, see above, p. 22.

Plate 29. Quaderno de algunas leyes. P. de Castro, Medina del Campo, 1544. Title-page. Reduced from 238 × 148 mm.

Pedro de Castro appears as a printer in Salamanca in 1538. Two or three years later he was printing in Medina del Campo for the local bookseller Guillermo de Millis.

The title-page shows the elaborate imperial coat of arms used by the bookseller and his successors in their official publications.

Plate 30. Episcopi Gerundensis Paralipomenon Hispaniae libri decem. Granada, 1545. Title-page. Reduced from 264 × 157 mm.

The press belonged to Sancho de Lebrija, the son of the great humanist Antonio de Lebrija, and was set up by him in 1534 in his house at Granada to print his father's works.

The title-page shows a form of the imperial arms, and grotesque and classical border-pieces, well adapted to the roman type, which the son of Antonio de Lebrija naturally favoured. See above, p. 14.

Plates 31 and 32. Yciar, J. de. Recopilacion subtilissima intitulada Orthographia pratica. B. de Nagera, Saragossa, 1548. Sigs. A 4 verso and C 5 recto.

Bartolome de Nagera continued the press of his father-in-law G. Coci, for

33

whom see note to Plate 7. At first he was associated with Pedro Bernuz; but after a short time the two parted company, and independently carried on Coci's press for another third of a century.

The first plate is a good specimen of a contemporary portrait—that of the Basque writing-master Juan de Yciar, the father of Spanish calligraphy. It is signed by Jean de Vingles, a Frenchman, to whose work, along with that of Yciar, the Saragossa press owes much of its fame during the middle period of the century.

The second plate shows a sturdy italic type—now coming into favour—surrounded by a border of printer's flowers.

Plate 33. Yciar, J. de. Arithmetica practica. P. Bernuz, Saragossa, 1549. Title-page. Reduced from 255 × 169 mm.

For the printer, see note to Plates 31 and 32.

The frame enclosing the title, although here found with gothic type, illustrates the changing style of decoration that accompanied the growing use of roman type in Spanish books.

Plate 34. Yciar, J. de. Arte subtilissima por la qual se enseña a escrevir perfectamente. P. Bernuz, Saragossa, 1550. Sig. K 8 verso.

For the printer, see note to Plates 31 and 32.

In this work—a second edition of Yciar's *Orthographia pratica*—ornamental woodcut border-pieces, signed by Juan de Yciar and Jean de Vingles, surround the pages of text, instead of the printer's flowers used in the first edition (see Plate 32).

Plate 35. Homer. De la Ulyxea XIII libros. A. de Portonariis, Salamanca, 1550. Fol. 218 recto.

Andrea de Portonariis was of Italian origin, and, like Juan de Junta, appears to have come to Spain via Lyons. In 1547 he appears in Salamanca, where he worked for some twenty years, while members of his family carried on the press for another twenty years.

The finely printed *Homer* is one of the few literary texts printed in Spain during the sixteenth century wholly in italic type, which in this case is French in style.

Plate 36. Pisador, D. Libro de musica de vihuela. Salamanca, 1552. Fol. vi verso. Reduced from 255 × 166 mm.

An elaborate piece of music-printing, done in the author's own house. The

34

page reproduced, showing voice part and lute accompaniment, illustrates a style of music book printed in Spain from about the middle of the century onwards.

Plate 37. Texeda, G. de. Cartas mensageras. S. Martinez, Valladolid, 1553. Title-page.

The printer worked at Valladolid for about twenty years, from 1549 onwards.

The book is printed in gothic type, but roman type is used on the title-page, the ornamental frame (of the same family as that shown on Plate 33) being better suited to the latter type than to the former.

Plate 38. Villegas, A. de. Comedia llamada Selvagia. J. Ferrer, Toledo, 1554. Title-page.

Juan Ferrer began printing in Toledo in 1547. He was associated with and succeeded by his brother Miguel, after whose death, about 1568, the press continued for some years under its old name.

The Ferrers printed a number of popular books in the traditional style. The title-page of a play here reproduced has shaded arabesque border-pieces which balance the title and woodcut they enclose.

Plate 39. Quaderno de las cortes (1532–1534). Juan de Canova, Salamanca, 1557. Title-page. Reduced from 240 × 160 mm.

Juan de Canova, the son of a fellow-countryman and partner of Juan de Junta, printed in Salamanca from the early 'fifties to the late 'sixties.

The title-page reproduced shows the adaptation of the royal arms for use with roman type. The printer's name appears for the first time in these plates on the title-page. Hitherto it has only been suggested by marks or monograms in border-pieces.

Plate 40. Montemayor, J. de. Los siete libros de la Diana. Valencia, [1559 ?]. Title-page.

This book bears no printer's name, but it was produced in the house of Juan Mey, who began printing in Valencia in 1543, and died two or three years before the present book appeared. Mey came from the Netherlands and systematically used roman type. With the arms of the dedicatee between the title and the imprint, the title-page approaches the modern standard.

c *

Plate 41. La Marche, O. de. El cavallero determinado. Juan Batista [de Terranova], Salamanca, 1560. Fols. 20 verso and 21 recto. Reduced from 148 × 104 mm. and 140 × 78 mm.

This work is really a specimen of a Spanish book printed abroad, for it consists of the sheets of an Antwerp edition of the poem, printed in 1555, reissued with a new preliminary quire by a Salamanca printer.

The woodcuts in the volume, which are much above the average for this period, are signed A, who is identified with the famous craftsman, Juan de Arphe. They were also used in a Barcelona reprint of 1565.

Plate 42. La regla y establecimientos de la orden de Santiago del Espada. A. de Angulo, Alcalá de Henares, 1565. Sig. A 5 recto. Reduced from 237 × 138 mm.

Andres de Angulo began printing in Alcalá in 1560, and worked there for nearly twenty years. He possibly learned his trade in the Netherlands, and perhaps for that reason was very successful with roman and italic types, which replaced the gothic types during his career.

The above book, printed for a famous Order of Chivalry, has several handsome decorated pages, as well as fine pages of pure typography in roman and italic types.

Plate 43. Monardes, N. Historia medicinal de las cosas que se traen de nuestras Indias Occidentales. A. Escrivano, Seville, 1574. Title-page to pt. 2.

Alonso Escrivano printed in Seville from 1567 till towards the end of the next decade.

The above work is well printed in the now prevailing roman type, with many illustrations of plants. The page reproduced shows the tobacco plant.

Plate 44. Index et catalogus librorum prohibitorum. A. Gomez, Madrid, 1583. Fol. 7 recto.

Alonso Gomez was one of the founders of the first Madrid press in 1566. He died the year after the above book was printed.

Early Madrid books are not generally very attractive, but the present work —partly in roman and partly in italic types—is an official publication issued by the Cardinal Archbishop of Toledo, and is exceptionally well printed.

The page reproduced shows the woodcut capital accommodating itself more and more to the new types.

36

Plate 45. Traslado de las constituciones de la Capilla Real de Granada. H. de Mena, Granada, 1583. Title-page. Reduced from 249 × 144 mm.

Hugo de Mena had been printing in Granada since 1558, at first with Rene Rabut, and afterwards alone. He was possibly connected with the press set up by Sancho de Lebrija, for whom see note to Plate 30.

The title-page reproduced is quite modern in placing a full imprint separately at the foot.

Plate 46. Missale Romanum. G. Foquel, Salamanca, 1587. Page 1 of text. Reduced from 254 × 178 mm.

Guillermo Foquel began printing in Salamanca in 1587, and later worked in Madrid. His whole career lasted only six or seven years.

Foquel's Missal is a well-printed book, contrasting strongly in style with the Missals in vogue during the first half of the century. Not only has roman type replaced the traditional gothic, but the newly introduced copper-plate engraving has replaced the woodcut. The book contains several large and small engravings, and the border reproduced will give an idea of the technical skill with which they are executed.

Plate 47. Salinas, F. De musica libri septem. Hæredes C. Bonardi, Salamanca, 1592. P. 308. Reduced from 228 × 139 mm.

Cornelio Bonardo took over an old-established Salamanca press in 1586. He died during the year in which the above book was printed.

The page reproduced shows the change in the style of music-printing. It also shows how successfully the printer grappled with the problem of setting up this rather difficult text-book.

Plate 48. Ribadeneira, P. de. Vida del P. Ignacio de Loyola. P. Madrigal, Madrid, 1594. P. 262. Reduced from 250 × 162 mm.

Pedro Madrigal began printing in Madrid in 1586. He died in 1594, and his business afterwards passed into the hands of Juan de la Cuesta, the printer of *Don Quixote*. He and Luis Sanchez (see note below) were the best of the sixteenth-century Madrid printers.

The page reproduced gives a sample of the printer's italic type. It also illustrates the influence of copper-plate work on the woodcut capitals, and more especially on the head- (and tail-) pieces, now coming into fashion.

37

Plate 49. Garibay y Zamalloa, E. de. Illustraciones genea-
logicas de los reyes de las Españas. L. Sanchez, Madrid,
1596. P. 6. Reduced from 317 × 227 mm.

Luis Sanchez continued the press set up by his father Francisco in 1572,
and became a worthy rival of Pedro Madrigal (see preceding note).

With its folding genealogical tables, this large volume is perhaps the finest
piece of elaborate printing produced in Spain during the second half of the
century. The engraved portrait of the future Philip III is by Pierre Perret,
who came from the Netherlands. He is known for his engraved plans and
views of the Escorial.

Plate 50. Devices used by the following printers or booksellers :—

1. Arnao Guillen de Brocar (see note to Plate 8).
Reduced from 122 × 81 mm.

2. Agustin de Paz (Zamora, Astorga, and Mondoñedo,
1541–1553). Reduced from 88 × 71 mm.

3. Diego de Gumiel (see note to Plate 9).
Reduced from 75 × 52 mm.

4. Guillermo de Millis (see note to Plate 29).
Reduced from 74 × 46 mm.

5. Jorge *or* Georgius Costilla (Valencia and Murcia, 1505–
1531). Reduced from 92 × 68 mm.

The initials in the device make a punning reference to the printer's name,
costilla in Spanish meaning a rib.

PLATES

¶ En este segūdo volumē comiença la continuacion dela primera parte del vita christi cartuxano ¬ prosiguese hasta el fin della interpretado de latin en esta légua familiar de castilla/por fray Ambrosio mōtesino dela ordē delos frayles menores del sacratissimo ¬ biē auēturado sant francisco por mandamiento delos christianissimos principes el rey don fernādo ¬ la reyna doña Ysabel reyes de españa ¬ de sicilia. ¬c. A honrra ¬ gloria dela sātissima trinidad ¬ dela muy soberana ¬ gloriosissima reyna del cielo nuestra señora la virgē Maria

E siguese primero el capitulo quarenta ¬ vno desta continuaciō que trata de como nuestro saluador alimpio ¬ sano a vn leproso el qual contiene cinco parrafos principales segū se cōtiene enel capitulo octauo de sant Mattheo ¬ enel quinto de sant Lucas: ¬ canta se enla segūda dominica despues dela epiphania/ ¬ los parrafos son los que se siguen.

¶ El primero es que los miraglos confirmā la doctrina dela fe ¬ la hazen ser creyda. ¬ Como el saluador sano a vn leproso. E que de cinco maneras cuēta la escriptura que fue curada la lepra.

¶ El segundo es q̄ el tañimiēto dela mano de Xpo es en tres maneras. ¬ E q̄ su virtud diuina se estiēde alas obras delos siete dones del espiritu santo. ¬ E que no fue menor la humildad dl señor en llegar al leproso: q̄ la potencia con q̄ lo sano. ¬ E q̄ por tres razones llego a el avn que lo defendia la ley.

¶ El tercero es dela razō por que el saluador mando al leproso q̄ callasse el miraglo. ¬ E de como ay tres maneras de mandamiēto. E que por cinco razones ēbio xpo a este leproso alos sacerdotes. ¬ E que el pecador avn q̄ por la contricion sea perdonado: es obligado ala confessiō sacerdotal. E q̄ la cōfession ha de tener ōtro cōdiciōes.

¶ El quarto es que por este leproso se figura el linaje humano. E por la lepra el pecado original ¬ es figurado el pecador por ciēco razones. ¬ E de como no tiene otro remedio el tal leproso: sino socorrerse de Jesu xpo.

¶ El quinto es que el que de sus pecados se halla limpio: deue ofrescer a dios sacrificio de alabāça. ¬ E q̄ tres cosas guardo dios para si mesmo que son/la gloria/la vengança/el poder dl juyzio. ¬ E de como el leproso publico el miraglo ¬ no peco. ¬ E dla causa por que el señor despues dela gloria d sus marauillas buscaua la soledad

¶ Siguese el capitulo. xlj

Ues dada la ley euāgelica eñl mōte: por consiguiēte se pone agora su confirmación por los miraglos q̄ luego se siguieron: ca del buen maestro es cōfirmar su doctrina por hechos esclarescidos: por lo qual se sigue enel testo. ¶ Pues como acabado su sermō se abaxasse el saluador dl mōte: siguierō lo muchas compañas: para hedificaciō ¬ consolaciō delas quales ¬ para la deuociō dl pueblo q̄ lo rogaua: se mouia a hazer miraglos. Sobre lo q̄l dize sant

ab ij

¶ Esto se cāta eñl domingo segūdo despues de la octaua dela epiphania.

3

¶ Titulo primero: como y en que ma-
nera los caualleros z fleyres dela orden han de demandar licencia al
maeſtre para poſſeer bienes z deſtribuyr z aỏ miniſtrar.

Ertenesce a aque
llos que algunas cosas honeſta
mente pzometen cōplir z guar
dar las mayozmēte que poz ſer
uicio de dios z ſaluacion de ſus
animas en religion beuir elige-
ron. Pozende los fleyres z reli
gioſos de nueſtra ozden ſegund
nueſtra regla que guardar pzo-
metieron no puedan tener pzopzio ni otra coſa alguna ni de-
ſtribuyr lo ſin nueſtra licencia. Ozdenamos z eſtableſcemos que to
dos los dichos fleyres dela dicha nueſtra ozden ſean obligados a
nos demandar z demanden li-
cencia para tener pzopzio z lo
deſtribuyr eneſta manera los
fleyres que andouieron con
nos en nueſtra caſa ocerca de
nos eſtouieren que nos deman
dē la dicha licencia poz las tres
paſcuas del año conuiene a ſaber Nauidad z paſcua de reſur
recion: z pentecoſtes para las
coſas que touieren z poſſeyerē
aſſi de patrimonio como delas
coſas que ouieren poz intuyto
de ſus perſonas: o en otra qual
quier manera poniēdo cada co
ſa explicandolo: diziendolo que
tengo de patrimonio puede va
ler tanto z lo que tengo de otra
manera tanto poz intuyto de mi
perſona tanto. Demando licen
cia a vueſtra merced para lo tener z deſtribuyr alos q̃ eſtuie
ren poz gran diſtancia que la de
manden dos vezes enel año cō

uiene a ſaber nauidad z pente
coſtes ſi pudiere poz ſi: ſi no poz
ſus letras enla fozma ſobzedi-
cha: pero que los comendado-
res mayozes que ſon fuera de
los reynos de caſtilla que la de
manden vna vez enel año poz
paſcua de reſurrecion poz ſus le
tras z los fleyres que eſtuuierē
enlos reynos do ellos ſon comē
dadozes q̃ la demandē a ellos z
q̃ quando los tales comendado
res embiarē a demandar la tal
licencia para ſi enbiē memozial
ſuyo z delos otros fleyres z co
mendadozes delas coſas q̃ tie
nen: los quales memoziales z
cartas mandamos a nſos cape
llenes que aſientē en ſus libzos
q̃ deſto les mādamos fazer: po
que ſi algun fleyre oluidando ſu
pzopzia ſalud no nos demanda
re la dicha licencia z alos otros
maeſtres q̃ deſpues de nos ver

b

4

Agni/fice di

gnitat? /mireꝗ
pietatis/ac pm
pte tuitionis vi
ris dñis Bernar
do çapila. Petro romei .Petro fra. Beré
gario lull. ꝛ Philippo de ferraria hoc an
no insigniſſime ciuitatis barchñe consi
liarijs. noīe ꝛ vice vniuersitatis: ꝛ singu
lariũ ciuitatis ipius: ꝛ eoꝛ. Jacob⁹ mar
quilles pꝛbyter minim⁹ in decretis bac
callarioꝛũ ciuis ꝛ incola ciuitatis cuius
supꝛa ꝛ in octuagenaria etate cũ vno cõ
stitutus nll'meꝗ obtinēs beneficiuz nisi
quandã in ecclesia barchñe capellaniam
valoꝛis septē libꝛarũ cuz dimidia barcħ.
vel circa. Salutē ac gradus vtriusꝗ salu

tis iuxta votum bone rei dare
consultũ. ꝛ pꝛesentis habeꝼ vite
pꝛesidium:ꝛ eterne remuncrati
onis pꝛemiuz cerniꝼ expectare.
xij .q.ij.c. bone rei. Vinc est pꝛu
dentiſſimi ac multũ honoꝛabi
les dñi/ꝗ cum antiquiſſimus
vsaticoꝛũ liber vestre ciuitatis p
clare insufficiētia lectoꝛ/ parte
catholica in qua oīmode ipsi
barchñ. vsatici seruantur p legi
bus videaꝼ tendere ad occasum
Cuũꝗ nature depꝛoperet nouas
edere foꝛmas que leguz laqueis
nõ sunt inodate. vt. C. de ve. suꝼ.
enu.l.ij.§.sꝛ q̃ diuine. ꝛ in feu.
que fuit pꝛma causa be.ami.c.i.
§.sed q̃ natura.coll'.x. Nõ est ad
miratione dignũ si vsatici fuere
conditi ꝛ barchñe tanꝗ a capi
te nuncupati qui nõ cõpꝛehen/
dũtur iure romano.Et q̃ omne

a

5

Capitulo.xxij.dela alteracion dela terçera figura mediante punto de diuision.

Eyendo tres figuras menoꝛes entre dos mayoꝛes perfectas ha uiendo en ſi el numero ternario ningunas de las mayoꝛes reci be imperficion como dicho es:mas ſi delante de la pꝛimera fi gura menoꝛ eſtara vn punto aquel es dicho punto de diuiſion poꝛ que diuide aquella pmera figura menoꝛ del numero delas menoꝛes y pone la en el numero de la pꝛimera figura mayoꝛ haziendo la imperfecta que de tres que valia haze le valer dos y con la pꝛimera menoꝛ ſe cuentan tres: y aſſi para dar complimiento al numero es neceſſario que la tercera figura menoꝛ altere como parece poꝛ exemplo Seyendo tres figu ras en ligadura dos menoꝛes y la terçera mayoꝛ perfecta segunda figura menoꝛ alterara.

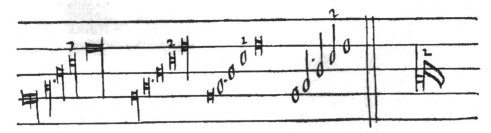

Capitulo.xxiij.de punto de augmen racion y de ſu operacion.

L punto de augmentacion es pueſto en numero binario para las figuras binarias hazer las ternarias . quando quiera que en la figura imperfecta binaria ſera vn punto haze la figura im perfecta perfecta . Eſte tal punto ſe podria y puede dezir punto de perficion pues haze de figura imperfecta ſer perfecta y no tẽ go poꝛ inconueniente que ſe diga punto de augmentacion pues augmẽta la figura de dos en tres:y tambien ſe puede dezir de perficion pues haze de figura imperfecta perfecta como dicho es.Muchos dizen y eſcriuen ſer tres maneras de puntos es a ſaber punto de diuiſion:punto de augmentaciõ y pũto de perficion:y ſegun la operacion que los tales puntos hazẽ ſõ dos maneras pũto de diuiſiõ y pũto de augmẽtaciõ o de pficiõ el pũto de diui ſiõ es pueſto en figura pfecta o entre figuras mẽoꝛes eſtãdo entre mayoꝛes como dicho es el punto de perficion o de augmẽtacion es pueſto en figura

¶Romançe del conde
Dirlos: y delas gran
des venturas que hu
uo. ¶Nueuamente
añadidas ciertas co∠
sas q̃ hasta aqui no
fueron puestas.

Estauase el conde dirlos
sobrino de don beltrane
Assentado en sus tierras
deleytandose en caçare
quandole vinieron cartas
de Carlos el imperante
delas cartas plazer huuo
delas palabras pesare
que lo que las cartas dizen
a el pareçe muy male
rogar vos quiero sobrino
el buen frances naturale
q̃ llegueys vr̃os caualleros
los que comen vr̃o pan e
darles eys doble sueldo
del que les soledes dare
dobles armas y cauallos
q̃ bien menester lo ane
darles eys el campo franco
de todo lo que ganarane
partir os eys alos reynos-

del rey moro Aliarde
deserimiento me ha dado,
a mi y alos doze pares
grande mengua me seria
q̃ todos se houiessẽ de andare
no veo cauallero en francia
que mejor puedo embiare
sino a vos al conde Dirlos
esforçado en peleare
el conde que esto oyo
tomo tristeza y pesare
no por miedo delos moros
ni miedo de peleare
mas tiene la muger hermosa.
mochacha de poca edade
tres años anduuo en armas
para conella casare
y el año no era cõplido
della lo mandan apartare
de que esto el pensaua
tomo dello gran pesare

FRANCISCO PETRARCA

con los seys triunfos de toscano sacados en ca
stellano con el comento que sobrellos se hizo.
Con preuilegio Real.

Question

de amor

De dos enamorados: al vno era muerta su amiga: el otro sir∕
ue sin esperança de galardon. Disputan qual delos dos sufre
mayor pena. Entrexeren se enesta contrauersia muchas car∕
tas y enamorados razonamientos. Introduze se mas vna ca
ça: vn juego de cañas: vna egloga: ciertas justas: ⁊ muchos ca∕
ualleros y damas con diuersos y muy ricos atauios: cõ letras
⁊ inuéciones. Cõcluye cõ la salida del señor visorey de napoles
donde los dos enamorados al pfente se hallauã para socorrer
al santo padre: donde se cuenta el numero ð aq̃l luzido exercito
⁊ la cõtraria fortuna de rauena. La mayor parte dela obra es
ustoria verdadera. Cõpuso la vn gétil hõbre q̃ se hallo en todo.

¶ P.V. Maronis Carmen de Venere & uino contra Luxuriam & ebrietatem.

DEO GRATIAS.

Et Veneris.nec tu uini capieris amore.
  Vno nanqȝ modo uina.uenusȝ nocent.
Vt uenus eneruat uires.sic copia uini:
  Et tentat gressus debilitatȝ pedes.
Multos cæcus amor cogit secreta fateri:
  Arcanum demens detegit ebrietas.
Bellum sæpe petit ferus exitiale Cupido:
  Sæpe manus itidem Bacchus ad arma uocat.
Perdidit horrendo Troiam Venus improba bello:
  Et Lapythas bello perdis Iacche graui.
Deniȝ cum mentes hominum furiarit uterȝ:
  Et pudor. & probitas. & metus omnis abest.
Compedibus Venerem. uinclis constringe Lyæum.
  Ne te muneribus lædat uterȝ suis.
Vina sitim sedant. natis uenus alma creandis.
  Sed fines horum transiluisse nocet.

DEO GRATIAS.

¶ P.V. Maronis. De Littera. Y. Carmen.

Ittora Pythagoræ discrimina secta bicorni
Humanæ uitæ speciem preferre uideretur:
Nam uia uirtutis dextrum petit ardua callem:
Difficilemȝ aditum primü spectatibus offert.
Sed requiem præbet fessis in uertice summo.
Molle ostentat iter uia lata: sed ultima meta
Præcipitat captos: uoluitȝ per ardua saxa.
Quisquis enim duros casus uirtutis amore

M

P.V. Maronis de Liuore.

Plecte truces animos: ut uere ludere possis:
Ponas mature bellum precor: iraȝ cesset.
DEO GRATIAS.

¶ P.V. Maronis de Liuore seu inuidia Carmen endecasyllabum.

Liuor tabificum malis uenenum.
Intactis uorat ossibus medullas:
Et totum bibit artubus cruorem.
Quod quisquis furit.inuideatȝ forti
(Vt debet) sibi pœna semper ipse est
Testatur gemitu graues dolores.
Suspirat.gemit.incuritȝ dentes.
Sudatȝ frigidus. intuens quod odit.
Effundit mala lingua uirus atrum.
Pallor terribilis genas colorat.
Infœlix macies renudat ossa.
Non lux. non cibus est suauis illi
Non potus iuuat. aut sapor lyci.
Nec si pocula Iuppiter propinet.
Atȝ hæc porrigat.& ministret Hebe.
Aut tradat Ganymedes ipse nectar.
Non somnum capit:aut quiescit unȝ
Torquet uiscera carnifex cruentus.
Vesanos tacitus mouet furores.
Intentans animo faces erynnis.
Est talis Tittij quod uultur intus.
Qui semper lacerat comesti mentem.
Viuit pectore sub dolente uulnus.
Quod Chironia.nec manus leuaret.
Nec Phœbus.soboles ue clara Phœbi.

Haec tibi pētadecas tetragonō respicit illud
Hospitium petri z pauli ter quinqz dierum.
Māqz instrumētū vetuz hebdoas innuit:octo
Lex noua signatur. ter quiqz receptat vtrūqz.

¶ Vetus testamētū multiplici lin
gua nūc primo impressum Et im
primis Pentateuchꝰ Hebraico:
Greco:atqz Chaldaico idio
mate. Adiūcta vnicuiqz
sua latina iterpretatiōe.

ϖάμτοθι Δἄγρομέμοιο Δυσαμτεῖ κύματος ὁρμῆ
θρυϖτόμεμος πεφόρητο.ποδῶμ Δέ ὁι ὤκλασεμ ὁρμή,
καὶ σθέμος ἦμ ἀΔόμητομ ἀκοιμήτωμ ϖαλαμάωμ.
ϖολλὴ Δἄυτόματος Χύσις ὕΔατος ἔῤῥεε λαιμῷ.
καὶ ϖοτὸμ ἀΧρήϊστομ ἀμαιμακέτου ϖίεμ ἅλμης.
καὶ Δὴ λύΧμομ ἄϖιστομ ἀϖέσβεσε ϖικρὸς ἀήτης,
καὶ ψυΧὴμ καὶ ἔρωτα ϖολυκλάυτοιο λεάμΔρου·
ἐισέτι Δϊθύμομτος, ἐϖαγρύϖμοισιμ ὁϖωϖαῖς ,
ἵστατο κυμαίμουσα ϖολυκλάυτοισι μερίμμαις
ἤλυθεΔῆρι γέμεια,καὶ ὁικῖΔε μυμφίομ ἡρώ.
ϖάμτοθῖ Δ᾽ὄμμα Τίταιμεμ ἐϖἐὑρέα μῶτα θαλάσσης.
ἔιϖου ἐσαθρήσειεμ ἀλώμεμομ ὁμ ϖαρακοίτημ,
λύΧμου σβεμ μυμέοιο.ϖαρὰ κρηϖῖΔα Δὲ ϖύργου
θρυϖτόμεμομ σπιλάΔεσσιμ ὅτ᾽ἔϜΔρακε μεκρὸμ ἀκοίτημ,
ΔαιΔάλεομ ῥήξασα ϖερὶ στήθεσσι Χιτῶμα,
ῥοιzηΔὸμ ϖροκάρημος ἀϖῆλιβάτου πέσε πύργου.
καΔΔῆρὼ Τέθμηκεμ ἐϖὀλλυμέμω ϖαρακοίτη.
ἀλλήλωμ Δἄϖόμαμτο καὶ ἐμ ϖυμάτω ϖερ ὀλέθρω.

Τέλος

Εῖυϖώθη ἐμ κομϖλούτου ἀκαΔημία, ἦμ ὁ ἅιΔεσι
μώτατος φραγγίσκος ξιμέμης θεία προμοία γαρ=
ΔέμαΛιος Τῆς ἰσϖαμίας καὶ Τολέτου ἀρΧιεϖίσκο
ϖος ἐϖοίησε , καὶ λογιωτάτοις ἐμ πάση σοφία ἀμ
Δράσιμ ἐμεγάλυμε, Δεξιότητι Δημητρίου Δουκᾶ
Τοῦ κρητός

 Areum opus regalium priuilegiorum ciuita
tis et regni Ualentie cum hystoria cristianissi
mi Regis Jacobi ipsius primi aquistatoris

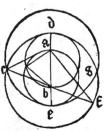

eſt triangul⁹ duorũ tātũ equaliũ lateru: & cuius oppoſitus angulus eſt extra
ſectionē eorundem eſt oīm inæqualium laterum.

¶ Vt ſit linea b a b e. τ deſcribatur ſup a puncti circulus ſecundum quantitatē linee a b c. item ſuper
b punctã deſcribatur alter circulus equalis ſcōm quantitatē linee b a b. τ inter ſeccent ſe in pũcto c. vl
cõ ꝙ linee a c τ b c ſunt equales: qm ſunt ſemidiametri circuloꝝ equaliſi: τ ꝗ a b linus ſit mino: eis:
pt3 q: dũ veniat a centro non attingit circũferentiã: ſicut a c τ b c. ergo eſt mino: eis.pt3 ergo ꝙ tri
gulus a b c eſt duoꝝ tãtũ equaliũ laterũ. τ ſic erit yſocheles. ¶ Rurſus ſit alius triangul⁹ a b f.et
ſit punct⁹ f extra ſectionē:dico ꝙ oīa latera ſunt inequalia:nã latus b f cũ ſit equalis b ꝑ. q: ſemidia
meter eiuſdẽ circuli:erit maius latere a b. τ latus a f.dũ ſit pl'ꝗ ſemidiameter equalis circuli eſt mai⁹
latere b f.nã a g eſt bf equale. q: ſemidiametri duoꝝ circuloꝝ equaliſi:quare oīa latera ſunt ine
qualis. ¶ Hunc ponam concluſiones de triangulo.prout eſt pars quadranguli.

Octaua concluſio.

Q: uiliibet duo trianguli in ſuperficie equediſtantium laterum ſuxta lineam
diagonalem accepti ſunt æquales

Eſt eni linea diagonalis que ducitur ab angulo ad angulũ: τ ſi eſt in quadrato: vocatur diameter.
fꝭ oſtẽdã in quadrãgulis ꝗ ſunt altera ꝑte lōgiores ſequaliſi lateriſi i quib⁹ min⁹ vꝝ. ſit ꝗ hmõi figu
ra a b c d.ducaſ ab ãgulo ad ãgulũ linea.c.b.dicoꝗ trianguli a b c τ c d b ſunt eꝗles.nã ãgul2 b ſupio:
τ angul⁹ c inferio: τ ſunt equales. q: coalterni inter equediſtãtes lineas a b τ c d. τ latera cōtinentia
iſtos duos angulos ſunt equalia:q: linea c d equalis eſt b a. τ linea b c eſt cōmunis:quare reſidui an
guli ſunt equales: τ tot⁹ triãgulus toti triãgulo equalis eſt ꝑ primã cōcluſionē hui⁹ capᵗᵇ.

Nona concluſio.

Si duo trianguli ſuper baſes æquales atꝗ inter duas lineas æquediſtantes.ce
ciderint: æquales erunt neceſſario.

Sint duo trianguli a b c τ b d e f inter lineas.equediſtantes.dico eos eſſe equales. Et ſiꝗ ſimiliter ca
dar linca d e inter equediſtantes ſicut cadit linea a b no eſt diſſicile arguere ex prima huius capituli:
qm anguli equates erſit a b c τ d e f τ latera tales angulos cōtinentia ſunt equales:qm baſes ſunt e
quales ex ipoteſſi: τ ſimiliter linee que inter lineas equediſtantes veniſit ſunt equales . τ ſic ſequiſ
ꝓpoſitã ex prima huius capituli.Sed ſi in triangulo a b c.angulus b ſit rectus: τ in triangulo alio
d e f angulus a e nõ ſit rectus:dico ꝙ tunc ſimiliter ſequitur ꝓ triãguli ſunt eꝗles ſi ſint ſuꝑ equediſtã
tes lineas τ ſupra baſes equales:diuidã eni ſuperficiē d e f duo media ꝑ lincã d m. τ ducã equediſtã
tes lineas equaliter e k τ f l. τ ducã c n equediſtãtē a b. habebo itaꝗ duas ſuperficies paralelogra
mas a b c n τ k e l f quas ſuppono eſſe equales. q: oīa latera ſunt equalia: erit igitur ſuperficies k e l
f diuiſã in ꝗuor triãgulos eꝗles ꝑ ꝓmiſſas: τ a b c n tñ i duos eꝗles:ꝗ duo de illis valẽvnꝰ de iſtis
ſed triangulus d e f cõtinet duos de illis:igitur eſt eꝗlis triãgulo a b c ꝗ eſt medietas alteri⁹ ſuperfi
ciei paralelograme. τ hoc eſt qõ volui oſtendere. ¶ Iſte noue cõcluſiones ad pñs de triãgulo ſuffi
ciant:quaꝝ noticia neceſſaria eſt in metthaphiſica τ logica τ naturali ſciẽtia apud Ariſtotelẽ.

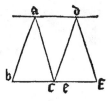

Caput tertium de quadrangulis:correſpōdens. 2. libro Eucli
dis:in quo primo ponitur vna propoſitio.

VNC dicendũ eſt de quadrangulis de quibus paucas ponã cõclu
ſiones:quib⁹ premitto vnã deſcriptionē ꝗ & premittit euclides li
bro. 2.de gnomone & de ſuplementis: vt præſciatur qd ſignificaſ
per terminos: & eſt talis.Omnis paralellogrami ſpacii ea quidem
que diameter ſecat per mediũ paralellograma circa eandẽ diametrũ cõſiſtere
dicũtur. Eorum vero paralellogramoruꝗ quæ circa eandẽ diametrũ conſiſtũt:
quodlibet vnũ cũ duobus ſupplementis gnomõ noiatur. Diuidatur ergo.a. b
c.d. paralellogramũ per diametrũ a d & in puncto K. in diametro:ſeccent ſe
ortogonaliter duæ lineæ.e.f. & .g.h. æquediſtantes a duob⁹ lateribus parallel
logrami ſc3. b. d. c. d. eritꝗtotũ paralellogramũ diuiſuꝗ in quattuor parallelo
grama:quorũ duo dicitur cõſiſtere circa eandẽ diametrũ.a. d. ꝗ diameter diui
dit i triãgulos.reliqua dicitur ſupplemẽta ſc3. g. K. c. f. & c. K. b. h. tria aũt pa
ralelograma.ſ. duo iã dicta ſupplemẽta cũ alterutro eoꝗ ꝗ ſeccanſ ꝑ diametrũ
gnomonẽ ꝑficiũt. igiſ hoc ſuppoſito cũ diſſōnib⁹ & diuiſiõib⁹ ꝑmi capᵗᵗ. hui⁹

B iiii

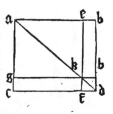

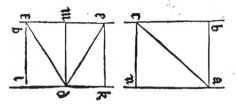

z los que escaparõ dela enfermedad murierõ a manos delos crtstianos: de manera que a penas ovo quien leuasse las nuevas a su tierra. E no dize la cronica dõde ni como murio este rey.

¶ Siguese la hystoria delos nobles cavalleros los siete infantes de Lara.∵.

¶ Aqui comiẽça la hystoria z muerte dlos nobles cavalleros y hermanos los siete infãtes d lara  N el año quarto del reynado dl rey dõ Bermudo q̃ fue enel año dela encarnaciõ de nro señor Jesu xpo de nueuecientos z setenta z cinco años caso vn alto hõbre dela hoz de Lara que avia nombre Ruy velazques con vna noble dueña que deziã doña Lambra muger de grand guisa:que era natural de Vigueña:prima cormana dl conde Garci fernãdez . Este Ruy velazques era hermano de vna dueña que dezian doña

Doña Maria.   Rey   Don Juã.ij.   Doña Ysabel.

Don Enrrique.   Don Alonso.

Doña Catalina.   Doña Ysabel.

Doña Leonor.   Fray Vicente.

16

¶Sigue se el tracta=
do. viij.dela phisonomia: en breue su
ma contenida.

Ssi como las
cosas frias se
téplá con las
caliétes:z las
caliétes có las
frias : assi se
curá y téplá
vnos cótrari
os con otros : y resciben medicina or=
denadamente. ¶Por semejante es vtil
buscar diuersos auctores. y maestros
por las diuersas sciécias : ca diuersos
siété cosas diuersas. ¶Por lo qual fue
nuestro proposito enel present en vna
breue summa declarar algunas soti=
lidades dela arte de phisonomia. De
la qual dize vn sabio : q̃ phisonomia
es sciécia de natura:mediante la qual
el docto enella cognosce abastadamē
te las differécias delos animales y de
las psonas en qualquier grado suyo.
E porq̃ qualq̃r sciécia es ó phisono
mia demos le eneste lugar su diffinici
on. ¶Phisonomia es doctrina ó salud:
eleccion del bié:esquiuamiéto ól mal:
comprehension de virtud: y desecha=
miéto de vicios.Esto causa el verda=
dero amor de dios : el temor del dia=
blo : la fe meritoria : la esperança del
galardon dela vida eterna que no se
puede perder : y el juyzio dela muer=
te:con la qual deramos todas las co=
sas. ¶Porque a ninguno aprouecha
en tal caso la sciencia : ni la potencia:
ni allegamiento de psonas:ni la gra=
cia dela hermosura : ni la voluntad:y

todo bien. Onde dixo vno. Todas
las cosas passará:yremos:yreys: yrá
los amigos y los no conoscidos por
ygual. Y en otro lugar. Todas las
cosas passan saluo amar a dios. ¶Por
ende fueron ordenadas las reglas de
sta sciencia y constituciones abreuia=
das:las quales son puestas abastada
mēte para lo que cumple: al jugo de=
las quales si alguno se sometiere aura
mucha honrra de mucha sabiduria
z virtud.Esto mismo le crescera mu=
cho el ingenio en sotilidad y saber.
La q̃l sciécia si touiere bié prompta:
y se acordaren della mejor entēderan
los dichos delos que les fablan:mas
cautamente conosceran los sabios y
los otros enlos veer z oyr quando có
ellos hablaré o ouieré de hazer algo
delante dellos:lo qual no es poco. E
con la industria desta sciécia ternā en
si gran parte delos consejos. y conos=
ceran los que les consejan como si sié
pre con ellos praticaran z touierá có
uersació en cada lugar. ¶E porque
enel principio dela sciécia de phisono
mia muchas razones y questiones di
uersas z marauillosas se hallan:ólas
quales ya arriba enel tractado dela
muger abastadamēte fue fablado:no
era necessario de recitar ni poner las
aq̃. y por esso solamēte comēçaremos
enlas cópleriones z q̃lidades zc.

Probemio.

Queriendo hablar dela do
ctrina dela phisonomia di
go que assi élos hombres
como enlas bestias:las a=
nimas y potēcias siguen el cuerpo. E

Carta de relacion embiada a su

S.majeſtad del Emperador nueſtro ſeñor por el Capitan general
dela nueua Eſpaña: llamado Fernando cortes. Enla qual faze re-
lació delas tierras y prouincias ſin cuéto que bá deſcubierto nueua-
méte enel Yucatá del año de.rir. a eſta parte: y ba ſometido a la coro
na real de ſu.S.majeſtad. En eſpecial faze relacion de vna grádiſſi-
ma,puincia muy rica llamada Culua:enla ꝗl ay muy grádes ciuda-
des y de marauilloſos edificios:y de grádes tratos y riquezas.Entre
las ꝗles ay vna mas marauilloſa y rica ꝗ todas:llamada Temirtitá:
ꝗ eſta por marauilloſa arte edificada ſobre vna grande laguna:dela
ꝗl ciudad y prouicia es rey vn grádiſſimo ſeñor llamado Muteeçu-
ma:dóde le acaeſcieró al capitá y alos Eſpañoles eſpátoſas coſas de
oyr.Cuenta largamente del grádiſſimo ſeñorio del dicho Muteeçu
ma y de ſus ritos y cerimonias:y de como ſe ſirue.

Palmerin de Oliua.

Libzo del famoso z muy effoz
çado cauallero Palmerin de Oliua z de fus grádes
fechos. Nueuamente corregido z hystoriado.

Las notas del Relatoꝛ cõ otras muchas añadidas.

¶ Agoꝛa nueuamẽte impreſſas ꝛ de nueuo añadidas las coſas ſiguiẽtes primeramẽte.

¶ Las notas bꝛeues para examinar los eſcriuanos.

¶ Carta de afletar nauios.

¶ Carta o poliça de ſeguros.

Nueuamente Impꝛeſſas en Burgos.

Año de. 1525.

creo tābien q̃ la aura de como vino aq̃ esa corona santissima: el rey dixo/assi es v̄dad q̃ la ay: p̃gūtado el como auie seydo: respō dio el rey todo lo q̃ la historia arriba ha cōtado dela v̄ida d̄ aq̃ llos sctōs ē marsella z mas hasta venir ala deuociō d̄la corona.

¶ La. XI. cuenta la manera co

mo la preciosa reyna delos angeles con su glorioso hijo y el san to esposo suyo Joseph huyeron en Egypto.

Uentan algunas historias q̃ piadosamente se pue den creer q̃ quando la reyna d̄l cielo con su hijo glo rioso z conel santissimo esposo Joseph huyeron en Egypto acaso enel camino estaua en vn monte vn ladron capitā de otros y este era padre del santo ladron que des pues fue crucificado con n̄ro redemptor. Ofreciose que n̄ra se ñora consu santa compañia passarō por alli: y este ladron capi tan delos otros les hizo mucho seruicio z tātas buenas obras como ael fue possible. Y recibieronlos en su posada donde vna muy buena muger q̃ tenia este ladrō hizo tanto seruicio ala vir gen n̄ra señora quanto le fue possible. Dizen mas que esta mu

Uiedo dela natural hy
storia delas Indias.
Con preuilegio dela
S.C.C.M.

Benedictio nubentium.

Bene✠dicat vos de⁹: cuſtodiat vos ieſus chriſtus: illuminet vos ſpiritus ſanctus: corpus veſtrum in ſeruicio ſuo cuſtodiat: cor veſtrum irradiet: vias veſtras dirigat: ſenſum veſtrū conſeruet: de diabolo vos defendat: z pducat vos ieſus chriſtus filius dei: ad vitam eternā. Amen. Deinde introducat eos in eccleſiā ita dicendo. Manda deus virtuti tue: cōfirma hoc deus qđ operatus eſt in nobis. A templo tuo qđ eſt in hieruſalē: tibi offerēt reges munera. Increpa feras arūdinis cōgregatio taurorū in vacis populorū: vt excludant eos qui probati ſunt argento. Gloria pri. Sicut erat i principio. Ad miſſam introitus.

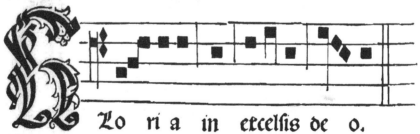

Enedicta ſit ſancta trinitas atcz indiuiſa vnitas confitebimur ei quia fecit nobiſcum miſericordiam ſuam. ps. Benedicamus patrem et filium cum ſancto ſpiritu laudemus z ſuperexaltemus eum in ſecula. V. Gloria patri. p̄. Sicut erat. Reiteratur introitus. Benedicta ſit ſancta trinitas.

Gloria in excelſis de o.
Et in terra pax hominibus: bone volūtatis. Laudamus te. Benedicimus te. Adoramus te. Glorificam⁹ te. Gratias agimus tibi: propter magnam gloriā tuā

Historias e conques/
tas dels excellentis/

sims e Catholics Reys de Aragó:e de lurs
antecessors los Comtes de Barçelona:com
pilades per lo honorable historic mossen Pe
re Tomich cavaller: les quals traines al Reverendissim
senyor Dalmau de Mur Archabisbe de Çaragoça:affegi
da la historia del excellentissim e catholich Rey de Despa
nya donferrando.   Any. 1 5 3 4.

Ab priuilegi.

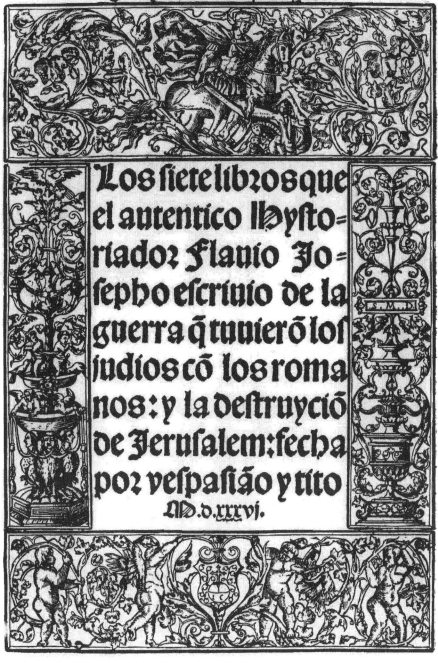

Los siete libros que
el autentico lhysto=
riador Flauio Jo=
sepho escriuio de la
guerra q̃ tuuierõ los
judios cõ los roma
nos: y la destruyciõ
de Jerusalem: fecha
por vespasião y tito
M.d.xxxvj.

¶ Primera part dla historia de Valécia
q̃ tracta deles Antiquitats de Spanya, y fundacio de
Valécia ab tot lo discurs, fins al tēpa q̃ lo inclit rey dō
Jaume primer la cōquista. Cōpilada y lo reuerēt maestre Pere Antoni Beuter, maestre en sacra theologia.

ANNO. M.D.XXXVIII.

℃Aranzel de los derechos q̃ hã de lleuar
los eſcriuanos de camara de los conſejos/ ⁊ juzgados
que reſiden en la coꝛte de ſu Mageſtad: y en las audien
cias ⁊ chancillerías de Ualladolid/ y Granada.

⁊℃on pꝛeuillegio Jmperial.

27

Aun bien no fuy ſalido de la cuna,
   Ni del'ama la leche vue dexado,
   Quando el Amor me tuuo condenado,
   A ſer de los que ſiguen ſu fortuna.
Diome luego miſerías d' vna en vna,
   Por hazerme coſtumbre en ſu cuydado,
   Deſpues en mi d'vn golpe ha deſcargado
   Quanto mal hay debaxo dela luna.
En dolor fuy criado,y fuy nacido,
   Dando d'vn triſte paſſo en otro amargo,
   Tanto,q̃ ſi hay mas paſſo,es dela muerte.
O coraçon,que ſiempre has padecido,
   Dime tan fuerte mal,como es tan largo?
   Y mal tan largo,di,como es tan fuerte?

☞ SONETO. ☜

El alto cielo,que'n ſus mouimientos
   Por diuerſas figuras diſcurriendo,
   En nueſtro ſentir flaco'ſta influyendo
   Diuerſos y contrarios ſentimientos:
Y vna vez mueue blandos penſamientos,
   Otra vez aſperezas va encendiendo:
   Y es ſu vſo traernos reboluiendo,
   Agora con peſar,y ora contentos:
Fixo'ſta en mi,ſin nunca hazer mudança
   De planeta ni ſino en mi ſentido,
   Clauado en mis tormentos todauia.
De ver otro hemiſperio no e'ſperança:
   Y aſſi donde vna vez m'anochecido,
   Alli me'ſtoy,ſin eſperar el día.

¶ Quaderno de algunas leyes: que no
está enel libro delas prematicas: que por
mandado de sus magestades: se mandan
imprimir: este año de· M̄. D. xliiij. años.

 Con preuilegio imperial.

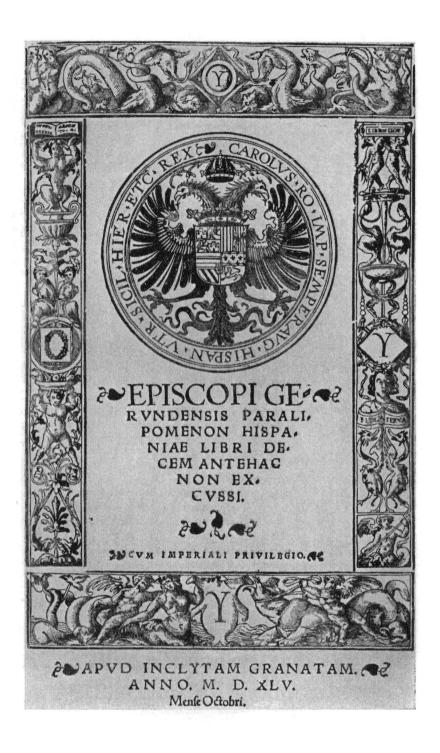

CAROLVS · RO · IMP · SEMPER · AVG · HISPAN · VTR · SICIL · HIER · ETC · REX

EPISCOPI GE·
RVNDENSIS PARALI·
POMENON HISPA·
NIAE LIBRI DE·
CEM ANTEHAC
NON EX·
CVSSI.

CVM IMPERIALI PRIVILEGIO.

APVD INCLYTAM GRANATAM.
ANNO. M. D. XLV.
Mense Octobri.

31

Escendiendo ala declaracion particular del talle y corte que se ha de dar a cada letra por si del Alphabeto Cancilleresco. Digo que es menester reuocar ala memoria aquellos tres diferentes tratos o lineas de que hezimos mencion quando hablamos del menear dela peñola. El primero delos quales y mas gruesso diximos que se formaua con todo el cuerpo dela peñola. Y el segundo que es el mas delgado y sotil se forma con solo el corte dela peñola. Y el tercero que no es tan gruesso como el primero: ni tan sotil y delgado como el segundo. avn que se forma conel cuerpo dela peñola como el primero. no empero yguala en latitud conel. Porque como el assiento dela peñola haya de ser ladeado alamanera que arriba diximos. tirando assi . ſſſ. vna raya de alto a baxo por el papel. claro es que no tendra tanta latitud la linea sacada enesta forma: como la del primero trato que se tira dela mano yzquierda hazia la derecha enesta manera. ▬

Esto assi declarado. digo que del primer trato y mas gruesso tienen principio todas las infrascriptas letras. a. b. c. d. f. g. h. K. l. o. q. s. ſ. x. y. z. E avn tambien la. e. segun Baptista Palatino. Todo el restante del Alphabeto. que es este. i. e. m. n. p. r. t. u. nasce del segundo trato sutil que se haze con solo el taio dela peñola.

Y para mayor y mas clara ostension delo dicho discurriendo por el orden Alphabetico. aduertiremos que la letra. a. se ha de començar conel primer trato gruesso. formando aquel punto de su cabeça conel cuerpo dela peñola : tirando dela mano siniestra hazia la derecha: assi. ⌐ y tornando ligeramente por el mismo puto hasta su principio: sin detencion alguna: descenderemos conel tercer trato: quãto al grã dor & cuerpo dela letra: assi ı. Despues de alli subiremos conel segundo trato que se haze con solo el taio dela peñola a cerrar vna figura triangular: que es esta. ɑ. & sin parar alli tiraremos de nueuo para baxo conel tercero trato quãto la longitud dela letra : dexan

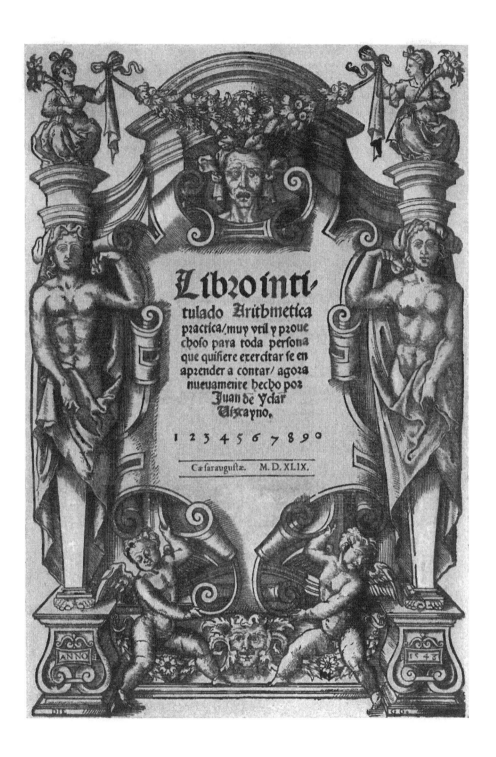

Libro inti-
tulado Arithmetica
practica/muy vtil y proue
choso para toda persona
que quisiere exercitar se en
aprender a contar/ agora
nueuamente hecho por
Juan de Yciar
Vizcayno.

1 2 3 4 5 6 7 8 9 0

Cæsaraugustæ.   M.D.XLIX.

ren de affentar los contadores el numero cinco (fe
gun el vfo comun de côtar) fean obligados a affentar a efta.v. y jamas a fu côpañera. En fu figura hay
alguna variedad, pero no tanta que fe deflemeje.
Exemplo, V.v.   ¶La. z. que quanto a fu legitima
poteftad no es letra, fino abreuiatura de dos letras
que fon. s d. fegun efta equiualencia en todo lugar,
principio, medio, y fin de dicion fe apofenta. Pero
en moldes antiguos, y aun agora enla efcriptura de
letra formada delos libros de yglefia, muchas vezes la hazen feruir por.m, y nûca por.n.como della
fuelen abufar algunos. Y es de notar,que jamas ella
fe atreue a vfurpar efte officio fino en folo el fin de
lapalabra.Y fegun ya comunmente defto murmurã
affi los efcriuanos como los impreffores, en breue
creo la echaran del poftrer lugar, quanto al dicho
officio.

❧ De la proporcion que en la
efcriptura fe deue obferuar.

A quarta y vltima cofa,que enla confide
racion delas letras y fu elegancia propu
fimos, fue la proporcion la qual es muy
neceffario guardarfe en general en tres
partes,es de faber enel grandor y tamaño del cuerpo delas letras, en los exceffos que hazê las que tie
nen aftas,por arriba o abáxo alos rêglones,y final-
mête en los interuallos o diftácias, que fon quatro

✣LIBRO DOZENO
de la Vlyxea de Homero.

Efpues q̃ la galera, caminando
Por la corriente, y ondas del
mar brauo,
Torno a la iſla Eea, donde
eſtaua
La caſa del Aurora y ſu
apoſento,
Y do naſcia el Sol claro y hermoſo,
Tomamos tierra en ella, y en parando
Saltamos de la mar en el arena.
Y alli nos adurmimos, attendiendo
A la diuina Aurora que llegaſſe.
Y quando vino ya, y moſtro ſus carros
Dorados, dando ſer a la mañana,
Mande que algunos fueſſen de los mios
A caſa de la Circe, y que truxeſſen
El cuerpo de Elpenor, que alli auia muerto.
Truxeronle: y cortando muchos ramos,
Hize que le enterraſſen en vn cabo
Muy alto, que en la mar entra y ſe eſtiende,
Con lagrimas de todos y gran pena.
Y luego como el cuerpo fue quemado,
Y las armas del muerto juntamente,

e ij   Hezi-

Emdechas de canaria entona
ſe la ſegunda en vazio.

Para ques dama tãto que   re ros

para ques dama tãto que reros para perderme y a vos per de   ros.

ros   para perderme y a vos perderos   mas

COSA NVEVA.

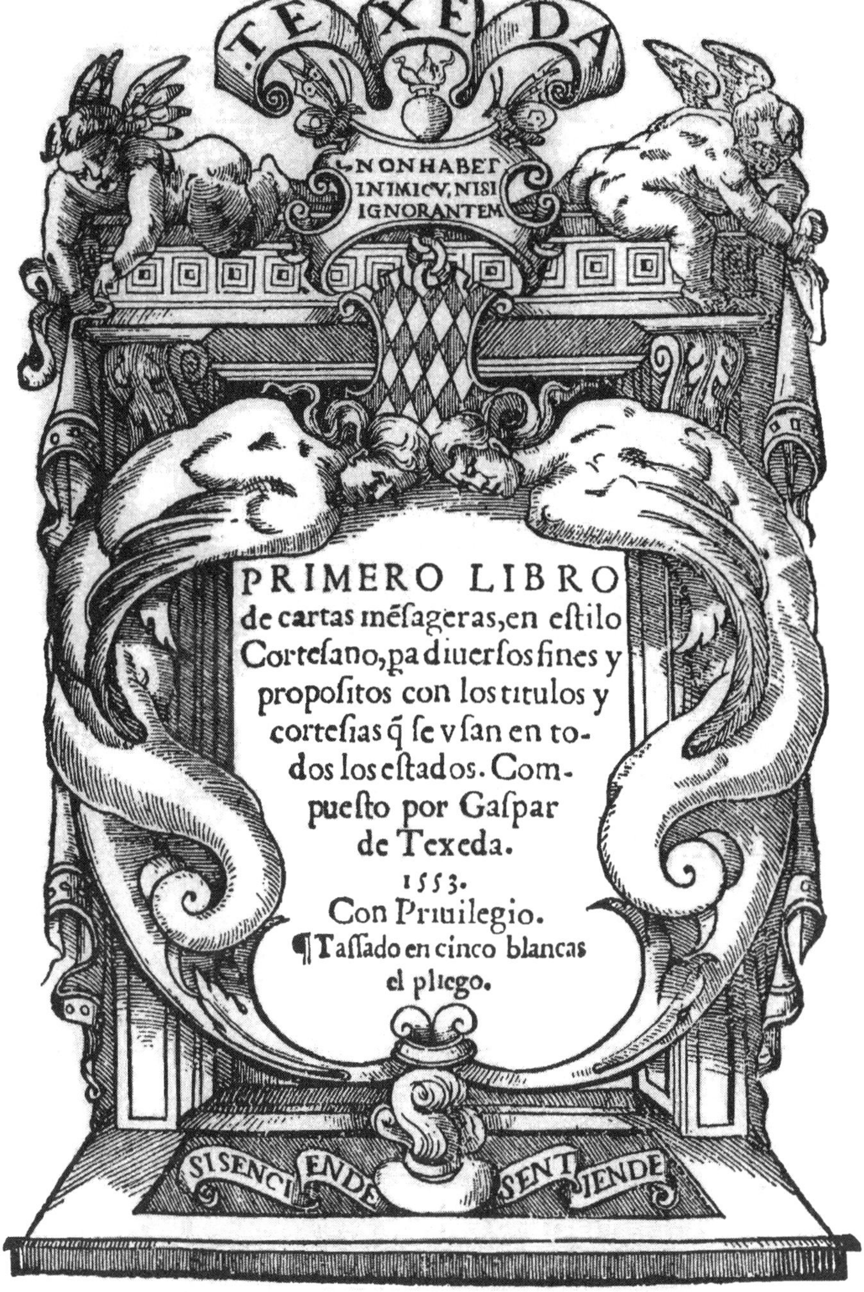
TEXEDA
NON HABET
INIMICV, NISI
IGNORANTEM
SI SENCI ENDE
SENT IENDE

PRIMERO LIBRO de cartas mẽsageras, en estilo Cortesano, pa diuersos fines y propositos con los titulos y cortesias q̃ se vsan en todos los estados. Compuesto por Gaspar de Texeda.

1553.

Con Priuilegio.

¶ Tassado en cinco blancas el pliego.

¶Comedia llamada Sel
uagia. En q̃ se introduzẽ los amores d̃ vn cauallero
llamado Seluago. con vna yluſtre dama dicha
Yſabela: eſetuados por Dolosina alcahueta
famosa. Cõpueſta por Allõſo de vi-
llegas Seluago. Eſtudiante.

✥ Quadernos de las cortes que su Magestad ✥
de la Emperatriz, y Reyna nuestra señora tuuo en la ciudad de Segouia el año de
M D. xxxij. Iuntamente có las cortes que su Magestad del Emperador, y Rey nío señor tuuo en la villa de Madrid, en el año de. M.D.xxxiiij Con las declaracio-
nes, leyes y decisiones nueuas, y aprobaciones hechas en las dichas cortes.
¶ Assimesmo la prematica de los cauallos que se hizo en Toledo. Con la declaracion
despues hecha en las dichas cortes de Madrid año de . M.D.xxxiiij.
En Salamanca en casa de Iuan de Canoua.

LOS SIETE

libros de la Diana de

Iorge de Mōtemayor, dirigidos al muy Illuſtre
ſeñor don Ioan Caſtella de Vilanoua, ſeñor de las baronias de Bicorb, y Queſa.

EN·VNA·FE TOSTEMPS

Impreſſo en Valencia.

27 Luego fuy derecho allá,
Y le dixe. Assi gozeys
D'el bien, que en el cielo está,
Padre, que me aposenteys:
Pues veys, que anochece yá.

El me dixo, Que yo fuesse
Bien venido, y que tuuiesse
Por cierto de ser tratado
En su hermita, y hospedado,
Quanto mejor el pudiesse.

28 El mismo me desarmó,
Y dentro de su aposento
Rico manto me cubrió,
Que para tal cumplimiento
La Prouifion se le dió.

Nunca assi fuy aposentado,
Ni vi huesped tan honrrado,
Como el que tuue al presente,
Que fué como propriamente
Pudiera auér desseado.

C 5

El Rey.

 IEMPRE hemos tenido por muy señala
da merced de nueſtro ſeñor entre las otras mu
chas y muy grandes que ha ſido ſeruido hazer
nos, por donde le damos ſiempre infinitas gra
cias, el auernos dado a entéder, como el mayor
cargo que tenemos pueſto de ſu mano es el
buen gouierno de nueſtros ſubditos, y la obligació que tenemos
para mantenerlo. Porque con eſto ſe cumple có lo que Dios prin
cipalmente a los Reyes nos manda, y por eſte cuydado ſomos
verdaderos padres de la Republica, y có el bué proceder de aqui,
merecemos de nueſtro ſeñor mas gracia y mas ayuda para exe
cutar mejor lo que eneſto ſe le pide: y todo redunda en mucho
augmento del bien publico, que quiere Dios ſe procure, y noſo
tros tanto ſiempre deſſeamos. Y aúque eſte cuydado del gouier
no nos tiene atentos en todas las partes donde es meneſter, muy
mas particularmente nos parece lo deuemos tener, có las coſas
que tocan a las ordenes militares, por ſer como ſon tan grá parte
de eſtos nueſtros reynos de Eſpaña: y tener como tenemos en la
adminiſtracion dellas el cargo de todo lo ſpiritual y temporal: y
ſiendo como ſon ordenes y religiones tan concertadas, es mayor
ſeruicio de nueſtro Señor conſeruarlas en ſu buen ſer. Y aſsi aun
que los años paſſados teniendo la adminiſtracion deſtos reynos
por mandado del Emperador mi ſeñor y padre que eſta enel cie
lo, mandamos hazer vn capitulo general de la orden de Sanctia
go con las de mas, que ſe començo en la villa de Madrid, y ſe aca
bo en la villa de Valladolid: mas deſpues que eſta vez boluimos,
de los eſtados de Flandes a eſtos nueſtros reynos, quiſimos ǭ mas
particularmente ſe atendieſſe a la buena gouernacion deſta or
den, por el deſſeo que tenemos de verla muy acrecentada en to
do buen concierto y religion: y por la neceſsidad que entendia
mos auia de nueuos eſtablecimientos, para la reformacion y bue
na conſeruacion dela dicha orden. Poréde Nos don Phelippe
por la gracia de Dios, Rey de Caſtilla, de Leon, de Aragó: de las

A 5   dos

SEGVNDA

PARTE DEL LIBRO, DE

las cofas que fe traen de nueftras Indias Occidentales, que firuẽ al vfo de medicina. Do fe trata del
Tabaco, y dela Saffafras, y del Carlo fancto, y de
otras muchas Yeruas y Plantas, Simientes y Lico
res, que nueuamente han venido de aquellas
partes, de grandes virtudes, y ma-
rauillofos effectos.

¶Hecho por el Doctor Monardes Medico de Seuilla.

DEL TA  BACO.

INDEX ET CATA-
LOGVS LIBRORVM
prohibitorum.

Libros que se prohiben en Latin.

A

B D I Æ *Liberini, ope*
ra omnia.
Abdiæ Prætorij, opera
omnia.
Abydeni Coralli, opera
omnia.
Achillis Priminij Gaſſa
rij, opera omnia.

Acta Huremberghæ: videlicet, Oſiandriſmus.
Acta Synodi Bernenſis.
Actiones duæ Secretarij Pontificij.
Adami Schuberts, opera omnia.
Adami Siberi, poëmatŭ ſacrorŭ libri decĕ ɛʒ ſex.
Admonitio miniſtrorum verbi Argentinenſium.
Adolphi Clarembach, opera omnia.
Adriani Barlandi, inſtitutio hominis Chriſtiani.
Ænea

TRASLADO DE LAS CON-
stituciones de la Capilla Real
de Granada.

(🙣)

Que dotaron los Catholicos Reyes don
Fernando y doña Ysabel de
gloriosa memoria.

Impresso en Granada en casa de Hugo de Mena.

Año de. 1583.

45

PROPRIVM MISSARVM DE TEMPORE.

DOMINICA I.
DE ADVENTV.

Statio ad S. Mariam Maiorē.

AD MISSAM.

Introitus 8.

AD te leuâui ánimam meã: Deus meus, in te confído, non erubêscam: neq; irrídeant me inimíci mei: étenim vniuêrsi qui te expéctant, non confundêntur. Psal. Vias tuas Dñe demônstra mihi, & sémitas tuas édoce me. ℣. Glória Patri, & Fílio, & Spirítui sancto. Sicut erat in princípio, & nunc, & semper, & in sæcula sæculôrum. Amen.

Quo finito repetitur Introitus. Ad te leuâ-ui, vsque ad Psalmum. ¶ Hic modus repetēdi Introitum seruatur per totum annum. Non dicitur Glória in excelsis. ab hac Dominica vsque ad Natiuitatem Domini, nisi in festis.

Orêmus. Oratio.

EXcita, quæsumus Dómine, poténtiam tuam, & veni: vt ab imminéntibus peccatôrum nostrôrũ perículis, te mereâmur protegénte éripi, te liberânte saluâri. Qui viuis & regnas cum Deo Patre in vnitâte Spíritus sancti, Deus: per ómnia sæcula sæculôrum. ℞. Amen.

¶ Ab hac die vsque

A   ad

46

Veritate cunffa faffa cerno,   Veritas manet mouentur ifta

Horum cantus erunt,qui & fuperiorum addito fono monochrono. Quintæ differentiæ
temporum decem & oƈto primum eft trimetrum cataleƈticum conftans duabus dipodijs
& dimidia & fono dichrono,dicitur etiam Archilochium,vt illud,quod affert Seruius.

Nox amoris & quietis confcia;

Et duo pura ex D. Auguft.

Veritate faffa cernis omnia,   Veritas manet mouentur omnia.

Huius metri eft Hifpana illa.

Caminad feñora fi quereys caminar,

Pues los Gallos cantan cerca efta el lugar.

Vt oftendit eius cantus.

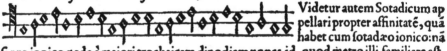

Qui cantus etiam quadrabit metris fuprà pofitis & fimilibus. Vocatur hoc metrum iam-
bicũ acephalũ,nã fi primam fenarij iambici tollas,fit trimetrum hoc,vt in hoc Horatiano.

Quòd fi pudica mulier in partem iuuet.

Nam ablato,Quod,reftabit.

Si pudica mulier in partem iuuet:

Cui fi adiungas.

Horna dulci vina promens dolio.

Poterunt vt Hifpana cantari.Secundum eft trimetrum acataleƈticum,quod & Sotadicũ
Seruius appellat,conftans tribus dipodijs integris,vt illa Aug.

Veritate faffa cernis ifta cunffa,   Veritas tamen manet mouentur ifta

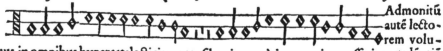

Videtur autem Sotadicum ap
pellari propter affinitatẽ,quã
habet cum fotadæo ionico:nã
fi pro ionico pede à maiori trochaicam dipodiam ponas,id, quod metro illi familiare eft,
fit trochaicum eiufdem quantitatis,vt in hoc ionico.

Palmam cape vicifti amor immerentem:

Muta duos ionicos in duas trochaicas dipodias,& fiet trochaicum hoc.

Palmam amor cape, euge, vincis immerentem.

Sextç differẽtiç viginti vnius temporũ primũ eft trimetrũ hypercataleƈticũ,quod fapphi-
cũ vocatur,conftat tribus dipodijs& fyllaba lõga,tale eft Latinũ illud,quod citat Seruius.

Splendet aurum,gemma fulget, fed placet forma.

In quo ob licentiam poëticam omnes impares,quos viciare non licet, funt trochæi : pares
verò fpondçi,quanquam inter fcazonta numerari poffe crediderim,cuius reƈtum erit, fi
ponatur in fine,Forma fed placet.Sed puriora funt & aptiora muficæ,quæ ponit Auguft.

Veritate faffa cunffa cernis optime,   Veritas manet mouentur hæc,fed ordine.

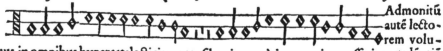

Admonitũ
autẽ leƈto-
rem volu-
mus,in omnibus hypercataleƈticis præter filentium vnici temporis neceffarium,pedé etiã
integrum voluntarium fileri poffe:vt quemadmodum prima dipodia cœpit à manus pofi
tione,ita & vltima in eandem definat;vt oftenditur in vulgaribus, quas Lufitani, Follias,
vocãt,ad hoc metri genus & ad hunc canendi modum inftitutis,qualis eft illa.

No

LIBRO QVINTO,
de la vida del Padre Ignacio de Loyola.

SCRIVIENDO la vida de nueſtro padre Ignacio, y continuãdola haſta ſu dichoſo tranſito, de induſtria he dexado algunos particulares exẽplos de ſus virtudes, que me parecio que leydos a parte de la hiſtoria, ſe conſiderarian mas atentamente, y ſe arraigarian mas en la memoria, y moueriã mas el afecto de los q̃ los leyeſſen, cõ el deſſeo de imitarlos. Y por eſta cauſa en eſte quinto y vltimo libro, irè recogiendo, y entreſacádo algunas flores de ſingulares virtudes, q̃ en el vimos, y conocimos muchos de los q̃ oy ſomos biuos. No quiero dar la razõ, porque cuẽto algunas coſas menudas, pues eſcriuo a mis hermanos y religioſos de la Compañia de Ieſus: que ninguna coſa del Padre a quiẽ deſſean imitar, les parecera pequeña. Eſpecialmente, q̃ no ſe deue tener en poco, lo poco, ſi con ello ſe alcança lo mucho: y en el camino de la perfecion, quien menoſprecia lo baxo, cerca eſtà de caer de lo alto: y por el contrario Chriſto N. S. nos enſeña, que el que es fiel en lo que es poco, tãbien lo ſerden lo q̃ es mucho. Y pues eſte mi trabajo ſe endereça a vueſtro aprouechamiento y conſolacion (cariſſimos hermanos) creo que os ſerá mas agradable, y de mayor fruto, ſi en contar las virtudes de N. P. Ignacio ſiguiere aquel orden que el miſmo Padre guardò en las Conſtituciones, quando pinta, qual deue ſer vn buen Prepoſito General de la Compañia. Porque a mi me parece que ſin penſar en ſi, ſe dibuxò alli al natural, y ſe nos dexò como en vn retrato perfectiſſimamẽte ſacado. Y no me obligo a dezir todo lo que ſè, y podria, ſino de coger algunas coſas de las muchas q̃ ay, las que me parecieren mas ſeñaladas, y mas al propoſito: para que

Luca. 16